Undercover Wildlife Agent

Undercover Wildlife Agent

The casebook of federal conservation officer Robert O. Halstead

James H. Phillips

Winchester Press
Tulsa, Oklahoma

One of the chapters in this book, "Isle of Infamy," originally appeared in slightly different form in *Outdoor Life* magazine. Grateful acknowledgment is made for permission to reprint it here.

Copyright © 1981 by James H. Phillips
All rights reserved

Library of Congress Cataloging
in Publication Data

Phillips, James H. 1940-
  Undercover wildlife agent.

  1. Halstead, Robert O. 2. Game wardens—United
States—Biography. 3. Wildlife conservation—United
States. 4. Undercover operations. I. Halstead,
Robert O. II. Title.
  SK354.H34P46   363.2'8   81-10324
  ISBN 0-87691-351-6   AACR2

Published by Winchester Press
1421 South Sheridan
P. O. Box 1260
Tulsa, Oklahoma 74101

Book design by Joy Flora
Printed in the United States of America
1   2   3   4   5   85   84   83   82   81

For Susie

Foreword

Since this book is about me, I think it would be proper for me to say something about it. The most important thing to say is just this: Everything in the book is true. It all happened the way Jim Phillips says it happened. I know. I was there.

All the same, certain names and even locations have been changed. In chapters recounting cases that resulted in no conviction, we've used fictitious names to protect the innocent. In this country, after all, a person is innocent until proven guilty. Occasionally, that principle of law can be frustrating to an enforcement officer. I'll be the first to admit that an officer can feel more than a little angry when he's sweated and maybe risked his life to catch someone red-handed, only to have the case thrown out of court on a technicality.

But I've dedicated my entire professional life to enforcing the law, and I'm not going to stop upholding it now even if it hurts. What the police sometimes call an "alleged perpetrator" and what TV writers call "the villain" is innocent until proven guilty. And anyone who hasn't been proven guilty isn't going to be identified as guilty in this book. Hence the fictitious names for some of the people who figured in my cases. That's that.

Some readers are sure to ask, since the book is about me—or about my adventures and misadventures as a federal wildlife agent, working undercover—why didn't I write it myself? The answer is, I'm a retired law-enforcement officer, not a writer. Sure, I can handle a few short paragraphs like these, but it's another matter to organize the events of a professional lifetime into a series of coherent, readable chapters. My thanks go to Jim Phillips for doing that.

There's one other thing I want to say here, and that's *why* I wanted the book written. It isn't just that I think my experiences might be interesting or exciting or entertaining to read about—though I hope they will be. It's more than that. I've spent my whole adult life working as a conservation officer, enforcing the wildlife laws. And I think the public should know what that entails. There are other officers, younger officers, out there working right now, sweating or freezing, going without sleep, sometimes risking life or limb, occasionally getting killed in the line of duty—and bucking a lot of government bureaucracy while they're at it. They deserve some recognition, some appreciation.

What they're doing is important. I think my job was important. Because the conservation of wildlife is important. Conservation these days is often called "environmental concern"—a nice trendy, high-flown, fashionable term for a fashionable concept. But to far too many people it's no more than that—just a nice, fashionable cause to which they can give a small tax-deductible donation. Well, conservation is a lot more than that. Among other things, it's making sure that a species of wildlife won't die out, lost forever, for lack of habitat or just because spotted furs bring a good price.

I think people ought to know more about wildlife conservation and enforcement. That's why, with the help of Jim Phillips, I've told my story—told it like it was.

Robert O. Halstead
Newark, Delaware
April 15, 1981

Table of Contents

Undercover Wildlife Agent

The Loon Hunters

It started with a rumor. U.S. Fish and Wildlife Service agent Robert O. Halstead heard the tip dropped casually into a quiet conversation on the docks at Morehead City. Halstead and a fisherman, who did not know Halstead's identity, were talking about hunting and fishing.

"If you want some real shooting, you ought to go loon hunting. They kill them by the hundreds. They shoot a lot of shorebirds too. It's a real big hunt each spring. Everybody around here goes out on it."

At first, Halstead discounted the report. It was simply another fictional story, he thought, a hunter's fantasy that grew with the re-telling. Most hunters exaggerate their prowess in the belief that a hunt's success is measured by the number of birds killed. Each time a hunter describes his hunt, he increases the kill. Moreover, loon and shorebird shooting was outlawed in 1918, a prohibition designed to protect birds whose populations had dropped so alarmingly that some species were threatened with extinction. And loons taste fishy. They eat only fish and aquatic crustaceans. The fishy taste of their flesh reflects their diet.

No, loons are not quarry for the sportsman. They are totem birds of the pine-forested northwoods. Their maniacal, laughing cries send shivers up human spines. Loons most often are seen swimming warily across northern lakes, silently disappearing beneath the surface when approached. The loon is a big bird with a long, pointed bill, a green head, and stark black and white body plumage.

Shorebirds are full of nervous energy, twisting and turning in swift flight.

1

Along the beach they spend their days scurrying ahead of incoming waves, and then turn around to chase the receding water back into the sea, a trait that delights and amuses sunbathers. Shorebirds comprise many species— knots, willets, plovers, curlews, and sandpipers, all with skinny, fragile-looking legs. All were heavily gunned by turn-of-the-century market hunters who sold them to restaurants. Tens of millions were legally killed before gunning was outlawed.

Perhaps, Halstead thought, the rumor was an isolated incident. A hunter or group of hunters had decided to relive bygone times by illegally shooting a number of shorebirds and loons. Perhaps it was this sort of one-time hunt that had been bragged about and described so many times that it had achieved local folklore status, an exaggerated tale of poacher's macho.

Halstead heard the rumor in the summer of 1949, soon after beginning his job as a federal wildlife agent in North Carolina. His primary task was to check waterfowl hunters around Lake Mattamuskeet, where the largest concentration of Canada geese along the Atlantic Coast gathered each winter. He also was expected to police the duck hunting clubs along Currituck and Pamlico Sounds. He was the lone agent in the state with thousands of miles of shoreline to patrol. No one mentioned the possibility of a loon or shorebird slaughter.

But the rumor persisted. In casual conversation with hunters and watermen, Halstead continued to hear the same rumor. Halstead found himself talking with anyone who would take the time, conveniently forgetting to mention that he was a federal agent. His discreet inquiries paid off. He learned new details that did not sound like mere rumors. From sparse facts, he pieced together a mosaic of unconscionable slaughter.

He learned that scores of hunters lined the Cape Lookout shore each spring to shoot loons and shorebirds migrating northward. Winging low over the surf, the slow-flying loons provided ideal targets for the hunters with itchy trigger fingers. Hundreds of birds fell dead under a fusillade of shotgun fire and were stacked in huge piles along the beach.

Shorebirds, he found, were shot throughout the year in violation of law. Hunters even set out decoys for the trusting birds, cardboard silhouettes attached to sticks that were poked into the soft sand.

Now, nearly a year after first hearing the rumor, Halstead was crossing the shallow waters of Core Sound under cover of darkness. Accompanied by ten state game wardens, Halstead planned to spring a trap on the loon hunters on Cape Lookout, a remote barrier island extending far into the

Atlantic Ocean, a windswept spit of sand where no law prevailed. At age 27, this was his first major federal case. He hoped his plan would work. He hoped the poachers would not catch wind of his surprise trap and cancel the hunt.

For the raid, Halstead had enlisted the help of George Hudson and Alex Davis, two Carteret County game wardens. When first approached, both confirmed what Halstead had uncovered.

"The loons move up the coast the first two weeks of May. Thousands wing past Cape Lookout. It's a very heavy migration," Hudson said. "For the poachers, the most important factors are the phase of the moon and the direction of the wind. A full moon means the migration is in full swing. An east wind is necessary to push the birds toward shore and within shotgun range. A west wind causes the birds to fly too far out to sea to be shot. The hunt this year probably will be held between the first and fifteenth of May."

"Why do they shoot the loons?" Halstead asked.

"Many people in these parts like the taste of fresh loon meat. It's especially popular around Harker's Island and Salter Path. Some even salt loons—like salted fish—to eat later. Watermen also want the wing and leg bones of the loons. They bleach them in the sun and cut them into 2½-inch lengths for fishing lures. The hollow bones are sometimes the only lures that will catch bluefish or Spanish mackerel."

Davis and Hudson told Halstead they would closely monitor the migration and the weather. When conditions seemed almost ideal, Hudson called Halstead, who immediately flew down to Beaufort from his home in Washington, N.C.

Halstead's team left the mainland shortly after midnight. They boarded the state-owned 28-foot boat, the *Clyde C. Patton,* at a secluded dock near Beaufort. Quickly casting off the lines and quietly motoring out into the treacherous shallow waters of Core Sound, they ran without running lights and navigated by moonlight to avoid being seen. By 1:30 a.m., they reached Cape Lookout and waded ashore. Hudson quickly motored back to the mainland, where he tied the *Patton* up at its usual mooring to avoid tipping off poachers.

On the island, Halstead gave last minute instructions to the wardens, directing them to spread out across the rolling dunes on the eastern-most point of the island. "Remain hidden until I stand up," he said. "That will be the signal to begin the raid."

The wardens silently disappeared into the pre-dawn blackness, scattering out before carefully concealing themselves in shallow depressions in the sand, in thickets of scrub cedar, myrtle bush, and sea grass. When all had found cover, Halstead looked toward the sound. He sighted an armada of advancing boats.

Small skiffs, clam boats, fishing boats, oyster boats and assorted craft advanced across the sound. The wakes from the assembled boats rippled like silver snakes under the bright moonlight. The sheer number of hunters was frightening.

The poachers anchored by the lee shore, picked up their gear and waded to the island. The hunters were young and old, middle-aged and teen-aged. They carried cases of shotgun shells, firearms, food and drink. Some were stoical. Most laughed and joked.

"We're gonna put the works to 'em," the ebullient hunters crowed as they trudged across the dune to the seashore. It was a scene from a Fourth of July picnic—hearty laughter, physical exercise, outdoor fireworks, food and drink. They trudged across the rolling dunes to the sea, forming a single file at the ocean's edge. Every hundred feet a hunter faced east, awaiting first light to begin shooting. The line of poachers extended along the beach for nearly 3 miles, the largest contingent of poachers Halstead had ever seen.

Shortly before five, the first faint touches of dawn illuminated the horizon, providing sufficient light to enable the hunters to see the migrating loons. The birds appeared black against a blood red sky. The hunters opened fire. The sound was awesome. A rolling barrage shattered the dawn, drowning out the sound of the surf. Hunter after hunter fired at the passing loons. One shot, two shots, three shots, four shots, sometimes five shots from each firearm. The reports were deafening.

Nor did it diminish. The migration was at its peak. A continuous procession of loons and assorted shorebirds flew past the thin line of poachers. Singles, pairs, small flocks, big flocks—all flew low over the surf, perhaps 50 feet from shore. The birds were driven northward by an age-old instinct to fly north to breed, to reproduce their kind. The loons never changed their northward course.

The intense gunfire took an awesome toll. Loons fell from the sky like autumn leaves, spinning crazily downward to splash into the cold gray sea. If a hunter missed a winging bird, the next hunter in line began firing at it. If that hunter missed, still another hunter would begin shooting. The poachers had erected a thick curtain of gunfire, forcing the loons to fly through a deadly gauntlet to survive. Most did not. In less than 30 minutes, nearly

3,000 shots were fired. Halstead, who had stationed himself in the middle of the hidden game wardens, stood up—the signal for the others to begin the raid and stop the slaughter. The wardens rose into view and walked toward the beach.

At first, nothing happened. The poachers kept firing, their attention focused on the loons. They looked seaward instead of glancing over their shoulders. They had posted no lookouts—they never had needed to before. Then the first warden was spotted, triggering an instantaneous response.

"Jesus Christ, it's the game wardens!" one hunter yelled.

The startled poachers reacted instantaneously. Screaming warnings to each other, they scattered in all directions, running like frightened rabbits. Some scrambled across the deep sand, scaling the dunes in a mad dash for Core Sound, where they hoped to board their boats and flee across the water to the safety of the mainland. Others ran across the dunes, hiding in shallow depressions or cedar thickets where they hoped to remain undiscovered.

But Halstead had planned well. Several wardens guarded the poachers' boats, cutting off that avenue of escape. Others chased fleeing poachers across the rolling dunes.

One young man reached a distant clam boat after a frantic dash. He jumped in the craft and whipped the starter cord twice. The engine failed to start. Seeing a warden closing in, he dove over the side into the water and began swimming for Harker's Island, a distance of nearly three miles. But he soon changed his mind and sheepishly swam back. One of the wardens had earlier removed the rotor on the boat's distributor, disabling the engine.

Hours later the wardens were still combing the dunes, finding hidden poachers who had fled on foot and who hoped to remain undiscovered. They knew their friends would return later to pick them up. The search lasted until mid-afternoon. The hunters were split into small groups and told to stack their arms. One or two wardens watched each group. The poachers stood on the sand beach at the high water mark; small clusters of men who smoked, made small talk and watched the loon migration continue. The birds that floated ashore were gathered for evidence.

The great loon shoot lasted for only 30 minutes. The toll of dead birds was frightening, even for the abbreviated hunt. "Nearly 250 loons were killed and another 150 crippled, birds which fell into the sea and were never seen again," Halstead said. An unknown but lesser number of willets, knots, and curlews also died in the dawn barrage.

Seventy-two men were apprehended. All pleaded guilty and were fined

$25 each in U.S. District Court in New Bern, N.C. An unknown number escaped. A few boys under age 18 who were apprehended were not prosecuted.

The great loon shoot was stopped. Thirty-two years after the birds were given federal protection, the poachers were brought before the bar of justice. Never again would scores of Carolina hunters join in the annual spring loon slaughter, an outlaw hunt conducted as openly as a Sunday school picnic. The Cape Lookout ritual had been broken.

The Early Years

Virginia Beach was a celebrated, wide-open resort town in the 1920's and 1930's. In spite of Prohibition, nightclubs flourished, and like many towns in resort areas, Virginia Beach had its share of gambling dens and prostitution. Located in extreme southeastern Virginia, the community was bordered on the east by Back Bay and on the south by Currituck Sound, where great expanses of marsh each autumn attracted legions of wildfowl. Wealthy individuals purchased extensive acreages on these marshes and established duck clubs to provide sleeping and hunting accommodations for the owners and guests. Throughout the autumn and winter, guns boomed across the expanses of marsh as sportsmen sought to bring ducks to bag.

It was into this world that Halstead was born on December 11, 1921. His father, Roland Halstead, was the supervising guide for a posh Back Bay duck club belonging to Ogden Reid, owner of the New York Herald Tribune. The elder Halstead's job was not unusual. Many local residents worked or guided for the clubs. The clubs represented an important source of revenue for many local families. But Roland Halstead was not content to remain forever as the supervising guide at Reid's gun club. He had greater ambitions, and in 1936, he declared his candidacy for sheriff. The declaration proved a turning point for the elder Halstead and his family.

Of all the local races, the interest focused chiefly on the office of sheriff. The race featured the elder Halstead, the incumbent, and a third candidate. The chief campaign topic was gambling and the illegal pay-offs to police and politicians who chose to ignore the wide-open games of chance. There was

9

considerable sympathy for cleaning up the town. Many residents loathed the illegal activity. They wanted it stopped. But when the votes were counted, the incumbent was declared the winner over Halstead by a narrow margin. The loss was a disappointment to the elder Halstead. He tried to mask his disappointment, remaining outwardly cheerful. But the rejection by the voters left him dejected.

And then a curious event happened. Several days after the results were announced, the sheriff was found dead in his horse stable. In the stable were boxes filled with uncounted ballots. Roland Halstead demanded a recount. After the recount, county officials summoned the elder Halstead to the courthouse. He thought he was to be named sheriff, to be declared the election winner. The Halstead family teemed with excitement. They could not conceal their glee, and anxiously awaited his return. But when Halstead came home from the courthouse, he was not the sheriff. He was a Virginia game warden.

Many years later, Roland Halstead explained to his son why he refused to accept the sheriff's post. "I was told I would have to accept bribes." As a sop, they named him a game warden, a job which immediately earned him the scorn of many fellow guides and local hunters.

The post of game warden is a curious one in America's history. To early immigrants, wild game often provided the sustenance of life. They believed it their right to harvest nature's bounty.

They also believed that wildlife should belong to everyone. Most of the immigrants were landless when they embarked for the New World. In England, the landowner owned the game and many of the impoverished immigrants had poached on the farms of the landed gentry to feed their families. The English gentry hired gamekeepers to arrest the peasants who trespassed on their estates and poached their game. To the poor, poaching was an honorable act; there was no criminal stigma attached.

One of the first acts the colonists did on arriving in this country was to declare the game the property of the state—not the landowner. Thus, a poacher who killed illegally was only stealing from the government—not the landowner. And government was not well liked; few cared a whit about the government's loss. Moreover, there was an abundance of wildlife. Few feared for the survival of a species or regional population of animals or birds. Game was plentiful.

When the elder Halstead was appointed to his post, the nation was in the throes of a depression. For many residents of Back Bay, the marshes provided a means of feeding their families. They baited ducks to make them easier to kill, they shot in excess of the legal limit, they often sold ducks to earn money. They believed this was their right, and harbored intense resentment against persons who thought otherwise. The game warden, like the gamekeeper in England, was the natural enemy.

Moreover, a few years prior to Halstead's appointment, a shoot-out between three poachers and several game wardens on Back Bay resulted in two poachers being killed and the third wounded. The fact that two of the poachers were relatives of the senior Halstead did not affect local opinion. Many individuals, friends and relatives alike, stopped speaking to Halstead when news of his appointment was announced.

The senior Halstead sought to blunt his ostracism by beginning an all-out public relations campaign. He arrested few persons initially; he talked with hunters and guides; he braved howling blizzards at considerable danger to himself to rescue stranded hunters. He sought to win their respect—if not their favor—before cracking down.

For young Halstead and his brothers, their father's ventures caused considerable grief. Classmates in school taunted Halstead, often picking fights with him. The game warden was the enemy, and the elder Halstead's sons knew it.

Halstead, however, was proud of his father. He frequently accompanied the elder Halstead on his rounds through the marsh. He learned to love the iodine smell of the marsh, to hear the wind moaning through the banks of reeds. After his discharge from the navy in 1946, he announced to his father that he, too, wanted to become a game warden.

His father objected. "I don't want you to suffer what I have had to endure," he said. "I don't want you to be exposed to the corruption of politics. Go into business."

But Halstead refused to heed his father's advice and Roland Halstead finally relented. With the help of his father's political connections, Halstead was named a Virginia game warden in 1947. Less than two years later he was hired as a U.S. game management agent by the Bureau of Sport Fisheries and Wildlife, the predecessor of the U.S. Fish and Wildlife Service.

Halstead's decision to become a game warden was a natural one. He had learned the art of tracking outlaw hunters at his father's side. It marked the beginning of an extraordinary career for Halstead, a career that would take him across North America in pursuit of men and women who plundered the nation's fish and wildlife. It would bring him into close contact with some of the best game wardens in the business—men like Chuck Lawrence, Rex Tice, William Davis, Dave Kirkland, Larry Thurman, Russ Gallo, John Wendler, George Ross, and Albert Sumrell.

Halstead often would find himself in great personal danger. He would see his investigations come to nothing because of political pressures exerted on behalf of suspected lawbreakers. Over the years, he would come to know the country intimately, and he would learn some bitter truths; that no species is safe from outlaw hunters, that national parks are not necessarily safe havens for wildlife, and that the killing of endangered species for profit or "sport" is widespread.

The Spawning Runs

The four men sat in a second-floor office of the federal building in Ketchikan, Alaska, above the post office. All spoke in hushed tones. Everyone was deadly serious.

"You must understand that if we fail," Halstead was saying, "if they discover you are spying on them, you could be killed. These men are violent. They could push you over the side of the boat and claim you accidentally fell overboard and drowned. They could say you were killed by attacking grizzlies. They could shoot you and dump your bodies in some remote area where no one could find them—and claim you disappeared. Anything could happen, and we wouldn't be able to prove a thing in court."

Halstead addressed his remarks to two college students. Richard Warren, a wildlife major at Humboldt State College, and Vern Sherman, a medical student at the University of Utah, listened intently as Halstead talked. The fourth man in the room was John Wendler, the U.S. Bureau of Sport Fisheries and Wildlife agent-in-charge of Alaska.

Warren and Sherman had worked in Ketchikan the previous summer as temporary federal game wardens, helping to police the salmon spawning runs. Both needed the money to pay for their college expenses. Now, they were returning for their second summer as seasonal employees.

Halstead sought to enlist their support for a bold and daring plan to apprehend the outlaws who illegally netted tons of salmon each summer, reducing the once bountiful spawning runs to thin remnants. He wanted Warren and Sherman to live in the bush far from Ketchikan, in a small backwoods cabin with the poachers and spy on them.

15

"You don't have to volunteer. We'll understand if you refuse. You'll be living with these men. If you slip up and get into trouble, we won't be able to come to your rescue. This is no kid's game. These men are deadly serious. But with your help, we think we can stop the wholesale poaching—and help save the salmon. Before you give us an answer, I want you to discuss it. Do it privately where no one can possibly overhear you. And then let us know."

Halstead's plan had its genesis from his work in Ketchikan the previous summer. He had been one of several agents asked to move temporarily to Alaska to help police the salmon runs. The seasonal reassignments are a common practice of the U.S. Fish and Wildlife Service which, in those days, was known as the Bureau of Sport Fisheries and Wildlife.

His arrival in Ketchikan in June, 1949 was an eye-opener, even for Halstead. Ketchikan's population numbered less than 1,800. It was a wide-open, hard-drinking, brawling port in southeast Alaska.

The port community took on a boomtown atmosphere with the arrival of the salmon-fishing fleet. From as far away as Washington and Oregon, salmon boats converged on the docks, boosting the population and sending local economy ever upward. Liquor flowed freely and fights broke out constantly.

The salmon fleet was attracted to Ketchikan for two reasons. Nearby streams were famed for heavy runs of spawning salmon. Pink salmon, coho salmon, humpback salmon, and chinook salmon homed in on the streams from the vast reaches of the Pacific Ocean.

But it was not simply the heavy spawning runs that attracted the transient fishermen. Several canneries were located in Ketchikan and they provided a ready market. Fishermen would load their holds with salmon, steam a short distance into Ketchikan to sell their catch to the canneries, and quickly head back out to catch more fish. In years of good salmon runs, fishermen made a lot of money out of Ketchikan.

Although many salmon were netted on the high seas, this form of fishing was often a dubious proposition. Schools would travel willy-nilly across the expanse of ocean, making it difficult for the fishermen to find them. It was much simpler to net them when they entered the shallows on their spawning runs.

The biology of the salmon is such that they are extremely vulnerable on their spawning runs. Prior to entering their spawning stream, salmon gather in huge schools at the mouths of the streams. At these staging areas, the salmon are easy prey. Authorities, concerned over the declining salmon runs, had closed many staging areas to commercial fishing, a prohibition designed to insure that sufficient numbers of fish survived fishermen's nets to swim upstream to spawn and renew the salmon's life cycle.

But conservation laws were widely ignored. The commercial canneries asked no questions about the origins of the fish when commercial boats unloaded their catch. The canneries wanted fish—and they paid hard cash.

Even the fishermen who complied with the conservation laws found it difficult to operate. These fishermen set huge funnel-shaped traps in areas outside the staging areas. The traps measured 100 to 150 feet long and an equal distance wide, forcing the fish to swim into a small area where they could easily be netted.

But the legal fishermen often fell prey to fish pirates. The pirates would simply raid the traps, scooping out the fish and transporting them back to Ketchikan to sell to the canneries. Some lawful fishermen posted a guard at their traps, often building a small floating shack to house the guard. The pirates paid little attention to any guard. They would fire a few rifle rounds through the shack to intimidate him, and if this didn't work, they often beat him up for good measure before stealing the fish.

This prevailing lawlessness prompted Clarence Rhodes, regional director for the Bureau of Sport Fisheries and Wildlife, to ask for more manpower during the summer to beef up patrols. Halstead was one of ten additional men assigned to Alaska for the duration of the spawning runs.

Halstead's first season was a revelation. Having been raised in a seaport community, he was familiar with wide-open lawless towns, but Ketchikan exceeded anything he had experienced.

Some salmon boats, he noted, remained tied up at the dock during daylight hours when most lawful salmon fishermen were at sea. These same boats would go out at night, and in a few hours catch a full load of fish, which they would sell to the canneries. Complaints about pirate fishermen increased daily, primarily from Indians who operated within the law.

Halstead also was puzzled by the disappearance of large schools of salmon in the staging areas at the river mouths. The schools would vanish overnight. This was especially disturbing because the staging areas were guarded by bureau agents and deputized employees.

During his first summer, the common gossip in Ketchikan's bars was that some bureau agents were working with the fish pirates to steal the fish. One name in particular stood out—John Lamb.

Halstead's experience that summer left him with the conviction that something must be done to halt the pirating of fish and poaching of salmon in the protected areas. He expressed his feelings to Wendler, and together they devised a trap to be sprung the following year.

The undercover plan, worked out in detail over the winter months, depended on the support of Warren and Sherman, the two college students. Halstead was already in Ketchikan when the students returned the following summer for seasonal employment.

"We think Lamb is working with Joe Patterson," Halstead explained to the youths. Patterson owned the boat *Rolling Wave*. Most days, the boat remained tied to the dock, Halstead noted, but Patterson still seemed to find plenty of fish to sell to the canneries on his nightly trips. Halstead, whose identity was known because of his work the previous summer when he arrested more than thirty-five salmon poachers, explained to Warren and Sherman that they would appear to be more susceptible to bribes. "I doubt they'd try to bribe me. But college students are a different matter," he told them. "What we want to do is assign both of you to work with Lamb guarding the mouth of Humpback Creek. All three of you will live in a small cabin at the mouth of the stream. We don't want you to let Lamb out of your sight. If he goes somewhere, you go with him. Give him the impression that you are not Boy Scouts who believe in the law 100 per cent. If you need to prompt him, shoot a seagull or two—something that's slightly illegal. But don't overdo it. He might arrest you in order to get rid of you. Sooner or later, we think he'll approach you and offer a bribe. This will be when Patterson comes in to net the salmon. Then we can arrest both of them."

Their only contact with the outside world would be when Halstead stopped by to pick up their grocery list, an event that occurred once or twice a week, he explained.

If Lamb was present and the students were unable to talk openly with Halstead, the grocery list would be used as a code. Two pounds of sugar meant nothing had happened. Five pounds meant Lamb had offered a bribe. Other foodstuffs and their quantity were devised to add additional information such as when Patterson might resume fishing, whether he had fished previously, how often he fished, whether Lamb was getting suspicious.

It was an ingenious plan—if it worked, and if Warren and Sherman accepted the dangerous mission. But Halstead's and Wendler's assessment of the young men proved correct. With little conversation and no doubts, the students reached a decision.

"We'll do it," they declared.

Halstead and Wendler spent the next two days with the students, reviewing the details of the operation, cautioning them on their behavior and mentally preparing them for the assignment. Then, after purchasing some supplies, they took the students by boat to the mouth of Humpback Creek, where a small cabin would be their home, and John Lamb would be their constant companion.

Two weeks before the salmon season officially opened, Halstead picked up the grocery list. It contained the code word "wheat bread." The students had been offered a bribe to allow the *Rolling Wave* to illegally net the salmon concentrated at the mouth of the creek. (Later, Halstead would discover that Lamb had offered to pay them $25 apiece each night Patterson set his nets.)

Halstead did nothing immediately. Instead, he and fellow agent Chuck Graham focused their efforts on other pirate anglers and poachers. They prowled the inlets and coastal waters with a zeal never before noted in the area—their purpose being to allay any possible suspicions Patterson or Lamb might have.

From the weekly grocery list, Halstead learned that Patterson fished the bays at the inlet to Humpback Creek every week. As the runs grew heavier, he set his nets two or three times a week. Finally, when the spawning season reached its peak, the students noted the *Rolling Wave* was fishing every night.

The time was ripe. Halstead and Graham decided to move in. They assembled two backpacks, each weighing approximately 150 pounds. The packs contained an inflatable rubber raft, a five-horsepower motor, gasoline, two sleeping bags, binoculars and two sets of raingear. A coast guard floatplane flew them to Humpback Lake, where they disembarked without being seen by Lamb. They waded ashore, shouldered the heavy packs and began the two-mile trek to the mouth of Humpback Creek where the salmon gathered in great numbers and Patterson fished.

The hike was arduous. Thick alders obscured their vision; they often could see no more than 5 yards ahead. The trail often seemed almost vertical. They sweated profusely in the humid air. The packs grew heavier with each plodding step, the pack straps cut into their shoulders. Suddenly, Graham stopped.

"We've got problems."

Halstead, who had been walking behind Graham, looked down at the trail. A pile of bear dung lay in the middle of the narrow trail. The dung was so fresh it was still steaming. The bear obviously was nearby.

Halstead pulled out his .357 Magnum revolver. It was, he knew, weak medicine for an enraged bear. If a bear attacked, it would occur so quickly in the dense vegetation the men would barely have time to react. The revolver would not stop a charging grizzly. "We should have brought a rifle," Halstead said. Graham, with a weak smile, nodded in agreement.

They decided to move on, quietly and slowly. They stepped gingerly over the bear dung, listening intently for any noise from the surrounding bush. Nothing could be heard. They began to breathe easier. Three more times on the hike they interrupted defecating grizzlies. The fresh droppings provided mute evidence of their presence, but fortunately, the bears remained out of sight.

Finally, they reached the mouth of the creek, took off their heavy packs and awaited the developments. They saw no one fishing the first night—only one boat entered the mouth of the creek. It cast a light around the shoreline and departed.

The second day, Wendler joined Halstead and Graham. He, too, had flown in to Humpback Lake and hiked the rugged trail. The three sat at the mouth of the creek, hidden by vegetation, and waited. About 11:30 p.m., the *Rolling Wave* entered the bay and began setting its nets.

A small boat soon came out to meet the *Rolling Wave*. Through his field glasses, Halstead recognized the man in the outboard-powered craft. It was John Lamb, the deputy agent for the Bureau of Sport Fisheries and Wildlife.

Within two hours, the *Rolling Wave* began hauling its nets filled with salmon. In the stillness, Halstead heard one of the fishermen cry out, "We got sixty-seven hundred fish. Not bad, huh?"

When the first light dawned in the east, the *Rolling Wave* had completed its run. It left the bay, heading back to Ketchikan to sell its illegal bounty. The three agents left later that day, hiking back across the rugged, grizzly-infested trail to Humpback Lake, where they were picked up by a coast guard floatplane. When they returned to Ketchikan, Patterson, Lamb and the *Rolling Wave* crew members were interrogated and placed under arrest.

After a trial, Lamb was sentenced to one year in prison. Patterson received a four-year sentence. He appealed. When the U.S. Court of Appeals upheld the conviction, Patterson placed the muzzle of a .30-30 caliber rifle in his mouth and squeezed the trigger. He wanted to live his life on the frontier—or not live at all.

The Duck Trappers

At first glance, Halstead knew intuitively that Henry Cofer faced serious trouble. Cofer, a young waterfowl biologist for the Delaware Department of Fish and Game, was normally a quiet and reserved individual. In the best of times, when he gathered with fellow workers after work to drink a beer and relax, Cofer rarely spoke. But now as he walked into the roadside diner, his movements were furtive. When he sat down in the booth across from Halstead, he only muttered a quiet "Hi," nervously fidgeting while waiting for the waitress to take his order for coffee. Cofer was playing with dynamite—and he knew it.

Cofer had requested the meeting in a call to Halstead at home the night before. Cofer had taken the precaution of making his call from a public phone booth. He did not explain what was troubling him. He told Halstead only that he wanted to talk privately. Halstead suggested they meet in an out-of-the-way roadside diner in southern Sussex County, where Cofer worked. If someone chanced to discover them, Halstead said they would claim to be discussing plans for banding waterfowl after the upcoming hunting season.

Halstead left home early that morning to complete the 90-mile drive to southern Sussex County in time for their 9:30 a.m. meeting. Now, he sat in the booth with Cofer.

"Something is wrong," began Cofer, who was in charge of duck-banding operations on Assawoman Wildlife Management Area in southeastern Delaware. "On a given morning I will catch 150 ducks. The next day I will catch only five to twenty—and sometimes none."

Duck trapping is a fairly routine procedure. Biologists place large wire cages in the water. The ducks are lured toward the cages with a trail of corn. When the ducks eat the corn outside the cages, they dive through a small funnel underwater to get the corn inside the trap. Few ducks discover how to escape. Biologists then net the ducks and place small aluminum bands on the birds' legs before setting them free. Hunters later shoot the banded ducks and send the serially numbered bands to the U.S. Fish and Wildlife Service or an appropriate state agency. By comparing the date and location of the duck's banding with the date and location of its death, biologists can obtain valuable biological information on migration patterns, how long the birds live, hunting pressure, and so on.

The major problem facing biologists during banding operations is luring new ducks into the traps. Wild ducks display little fear of returning to a trap where they have been banded and released. Indeed, the allure of corn is so strong that banded ducks often flock to a trap like chickadees to a backyard bird feeder. Biologists soon discover that nearly all the birds in a trap are wearing aluminum bands. At this point, banding operations are halted. All the ducks in the area have been tagged.

Cofer, however, was not facing this problem. His birds were disappearing. On days the traps are nearly devoid of birds, he told Halstead, "The water will be muddy, the corn gone and the trap filled with feathers." Clearly, the ducks had been in the trap. They had stirred up the bottom muck diving for the corn. They had eaten the corn, and the feathers floating on the surface were mute evidence of their presence. "The ducks are being stolen before I arrive in the morning to begin banding," Cofer said.

Cofer's disclosure was not Halstead's first inkling of trap thefts. Another Delaware biologist who had missed a number of ducks in his traps had talked to Halstead. And a charter boat captain with whom Halstead fished had heard stories about the Assawoman theft operation. He, too, quietly alerted Halstead. Neither of them knew much about the operation. But Cofer was no ordinary tipster.

"Who do you think is doing it?" Halstead asked.

Cofer took a deep breath. His hand clutched a coffee cup. He first glanced down at the table top and then looked up at Halstead.

"Horace Mitchell, the assistant refuge manager for Assawoman," he replied. "And I believe one of the Delaware dog wardens is helping Mitchell."

Duck banding would not begin for several months; not until the gunning season ended in mid-January. But Cofer was worried the thefts would continue. "I hope you will help me when I begin banding," he pleaded.

It was not an idle request. The Delaware Department of Fish and Game was rife with politics. If word leaked that Cofer was actively helping a federal man, powerful politicians would ensure that he would immediately be fired. Many State Fish and Game employees had been fired for less—and Mitchell, the assistant refuge manager, had friends who were powerful and influential politicians.

Cofer also added a warning. "These people watch Russ Gallo's movements closely; therefore I suggest he should remain at home and not come into this." Russell Gallo was Halstead's partner in Delaware. The federal agent lived in Dover and often worked in Sussex County, including the Assawoman area. Halstead would have to spearhead the investigation from Newark. "I'll call you when I begin missing ducks," Cofer said. "You take it from there."

Nearly three months passed. Halstead made no inquiries, dropped no hints to anyone that he was aware of the trap thefts. He bided his time, waiting for the gunning season to end and duck banding operations to begin.

Late in the day on January 29, nine days after the duck season ended in 1967, his phone rang. It was Gordon Nightingale, manager of the Bombay Hook National Wildlife Refuge and a close friend of Cofer's. "Tomorrow morning will be the day," Nightingale said. "Henry Cofer wanted me to tell you that." Cofer was cautious. His first call was made from a pay phone. His second was relayed via a mutual friend. He covered his tracks well. But with his job at stake, he could not be too careful.

Less than four hours later, Halstead was on the road, driving through a gathering snowstorm to Bombay Hook National Wildlife Refuge, about 35 miles southeast of Newark.

Halstead decided to drive first to the refuge to pick up Nightingale and Dale Coggeshall, an assistant refuge manager. Cofer's warning that the poachers kept Gallo (the federal game agent who lived in Dover) under surveillance—a not uncommon practice among poachers—eliminated him. Both Nightingale and Coggeshall were deputized federal law enforcement officers. (Although most people are not aware of it, most national wildlife refuge employees are deputized. This enables them to arrest persons violating refuge regulations.)

At midnight Halstead left the refuge with Nightingale and Coggeshall. The snowstorm was developing into a near blizzard. The mercury plummeted. The northwest winds shrieked across the landscape. Heavy snow blanketed the fields and woods. Visibility was near zero as the trio drove south toward Assawoman Wildlife Management area.

Located on the western shore of Assawoman Bay, the wildlife area consists of a sprawling tidal marsh with mile after mile of shallow brackish flats and banks of tan marsh grass. Clumps of loblolly pine and hardwoods rise from highland areas, breaking up the monotonous expanse of marsh grass. The marsh is intersected with dikes, which the state built to create freshwater ponds for wintering wildfowl. Roads run along the tops of the dikes and are used commonly by local hunters, fishermen and refuge personnel.

"I doubt we have any luck," Halstead told his companions. "This weather will probably freeze the shallow flats where the traps are set. I doubt any ducks will come in."

Nevertheless, Halstead pressed on. The car's heater was set on high as he drove through the darkness. The windshield wipers, heavily encrusted with ice, clacked against the cold glass. About 3 a.m. the trio reached the wildlife area. Two routes led to the area where the traps were located. One was impassable. They would have to walk on foot across miles of tidal flat and marsh—a long, treacherous journey in mild weather. With the snowstorm, the arduous journey was out of the question. A man could die of exposure.

The second route offered the best chance for the trio to be spotted by the poachers, but Halstead had no other choice. He turned left off the highway and drove northward along the main entrance road to the wildlife area. But instead of turning right toward the headquarters building, Halstead continued straight for some distance. He parked the car in a small woods, where he hoped it would remain hidden from view.

"Nightingale and I will check out the traps. You stay with the car," Halstead told Coggeshall. "If we find open water and ducks are in the traps, we'll begin a stakeout. If not, we'll return."

Bundled in heavy down coats and insulated hip-boots, they began their trek. Before they had walked 30 yards, Nightingale asked, "How will we hide our tracks?" Their footprints sank deep into the freshly fallen snow.

"Let's hope more snow covers them before Mitchell awakens," replied Halstead.

They walked nearly a mile through the blowing snow before coming to the clearing where refuge headquarters and Mitchell's house-trailer were located. Mitchell, the assistant manager of the refuge, owned a dog that barked at the slightest provocation. But the only passable route to the traps required them to walk past the clearing where the trailer was parked. Without uttering a sound, the pair crept across the clearing. Only the soft crunch of snow underfoot betrayed their presence. Mitchell's dog did not bark.

For the next ninety minutes, Halstead and Nightingale braved the storm. They plodded across dike and tidal marsh, looking for the duck traps. The cold was numbing. The howling winds gathered strength; windblown snow stung their faces. Finally, they found the cove where Cofer had set his traps. In the darkness, they broke through the thin ice as they made their way across the shallows to the biggest trap. No ducks were present. The ice had frozen the water surface completely. Another nearby trap set in deeper water also was frozen over. They moved toward the last trap. When Halstead first glimpsed the trap through the heavily falling snow, he saw more than fifteen canvasbacks nervously swimming back and forth to circulate the water and keep ice from forming. He could make out the drakes' russet colored heads, black breasts, white flanks, and wedge-shaped bills.

Halstead radioed Coggeshall, who was waiting in the car. "We found some ducks. We'll stay here past dawn," he said.

Halstead and Nightingale walked 100 yards away to a tangle of marsh grass and myrtle bush. It was the only cover available. They crawled into the grass and waited.

Two hours passed. The storm raged, dumping two more inches of snow, covering their tracks. Both men were shivering and exhausted. Finally, when they were nearly blue with cold, Halstead spotted a pick-up truck approaching.

"Here he comes," Halstead whispered.

Mitchell approached the traps warily. He drove only short distances along the dike, stopping frequently. Rolling down his window, he glanced out at the surrounding countryside, looking for signs of intruders. He looked across the tidal flats. He probed nearby woods with field glasses.

Finally, apparently satisfied that nothing was amiss, he stopped his pick-up on the dike close to the traps. He got out and removed a small cage and long-handled net from the back of his truck. Breaking through the thin ice, he waded out to the trap containing the canvasbacks.

The ducks fluttered and crashed in flight against the wire cage when Mitchell approached. They sought escape, but failed, falling back into the water after hitting the wire. Mitchell quickly opened a small wire door, scooped up the frightened fowl with his long-handled net and placed the birds in the small cage. Within minutes, he had netted all the ducks. He walked back to the dike, placed the caged ducks in the bed of the pick-up truck and drove off. His efforts took less than ten minutes.

Halstead responded instantly. He pulled his walkie-talkie from his coat pocket, pressed the button and spoke into the microphone. There was no answer from Coggeshall. He yelled into the microphone, "Dale, can you copy?" No answer.

"The goddam batteries are frozen!"

Thinking quickly, he pushed the radio under his down coat and pressed it against his skin. Precious minutes elapsed while the batteries warmed. Finally, he made radio contact.

Coggeshall, meanwhile, had left Halstead's car and walked through the woods to the edge of the clearing where Mitchell's house-trailer was located. He watched Mitchell return.

"Mitchell came back to his trailer and gave the ducks to another man waiting in a pick-up," Coggeshall told Halstead by radio.

"Watch the pick-up with the ducks," Halstead said. "When it leaves, follow it. If you can't follow it because of the roads, use my red light and pull him over and wait for us." Halstead was worried. He wanted to follow the second pick-up to its final destination. This would tell him where the ducks were being sent. But now he had little choice.

Immediately, the exhausted Halstead and Nightingale plunged through the deep, drifting snow and ran up on the dike. They trotted along the dike road toward Mitchell's trailer, following the tracks left by Mitchell's pick-up. The trailer was nearly three miles distant. Halstead doubted he would reach it before the second pick-up departed.

He was right. The second pick-up left almost immediately, but not before Coggeshall had returned to Halstead's car. Coggeshall followed the second pick-up out of the Assawoman Wildlife Area onto a road leading toward Ocean Vie, a nearby town. But the roads were too hazardous, the snow was too deep. Coggeshall became worried he would lose sight of the vehicle. He decided to stop the pick-up. He turned on the red flashing light and pulled over the pick-up. It was driven by Lloyd Hickman, a state dog warden. In the back of the pick-up was a gunny sack containing sixteen dead canvasbacks.

Both men later pleaded guilty before a U.S. magistrate. Mitchell was fined $450 for trapping ducks. Hickman was fined $25 for illegally transporting ducks. The fines were paid by an influential Delaware state senator from Sussex County. Mitchell was suspended from his job and Hickman was suspended but later reinstated as dog warden with the Department of Fish and Game, the agency whose responsibility includes protecting waterfowl. Among those who spear-headed the fight to prevent Hickman's dismissal was the senator who paid the fines.

Halstead believed the trapped ducks were given to local politicians, or sold in Baltimore.

During the investigation which followed the arrests, Cofer's name never surfaced. The man who triggered the probe, who placed his job on the line, remained anonymous. The youthful Cofer died several years later.

The Big Fish That Got Away

Alton Hoover and Haines Campbell, not their real names, are hard-drinking, rough-hewn men who mask their inner toughness with a joking, backslapping joviality. To passengers waiting in the Toledo, Ohio airport, the locker-room banter of the two men disguised their deep suspicions about the two individuals they were to meet on the noon flight from Baltimore. One had identified himself in a telephone conversation as a Rex Huggins, who said he wanted to purchase freshly-caught walleyes and yellow perch. The request piqued their curiosity: how did these men from the East Coast obtain their names as marketeers of illegally-netted fish?

Huggins was Halstead, who posed as a representative of the S.D. Seafood Co. of Piney Point, Maryland. Halstead had said in telephone conversations with Hoover that the firm wanted to discuss buying walleye fillets to sell to restaurants on the mid-Atlantic seaboard. He added that he would bring with him the firm's president, John Stone.

When they stepped off the plane and introduced themselves, Hoover suggested they go downtown to eat. "The food here is no good," he explained.

Halstead agreed to the suggestion, and the four men walked out of the terminal to the parking lot, casually bantering about the warm spring weather, the flight from Baltimore and the miseries of air travel. When they arrived at Campbell's auto, Halstead and Stone sat in the back seat. Hoover and Campbell occupied the front. No sooner had they driven out of the parking lot onto the highway than Hoover turned around, glared at Halstead and asked, "Where did you get our names?"

31

"I started calling fish processing houses," Halstead said. "A woman I know who works at a fish company said we should talk to you, that you might be able to help us out." The answer did not satisfy Hoover. He continued glaring, never taking his eyes off Halstead. Halstead also mentioned the name of a bartender at a tavern the two men frequented. "If anybody in this area knew how to get fish, he said it would be you two. And a couple of guys drinking at the bar added that he was right."

Hoover's eyes suddenly lit up. He chuckled. Campbell chuckled. Suddenly, both men in the front seat were laughing uproariously. Halstead's answer struck both men as exceedingly funny. The tavern was their favorite hangout. They knew the bartender, they knew the patrons. They had inordinate trust in their drinking companions and there were few secrets among the regulars. The tavern was their home away from home. And now their fun-loving drinking buddies were referring *business* to them! It struck them as hilarious. The tension drained from their faces. These men—this Huggins and Stone—were okay.

Halstead had done it again. He had erased the doubts of a suspicious man. He wanted to buy fish. More specifically, he wanted to purchase walleyes and yellow perch—species believed to be illegally netted in the Great Lakes. Halstead had established the S.D. Seafood Company to provide himself with a facility capable of handling what he hoped would be *tons* of fish. He did not seek the weekend poacher who occasionally sells a fish here or a few pounds there. He wanted to snare the wholesale commercial poachers who systematically plunder the Great Lakes of their treasures.

His companion was John Stone, a restaurateur and steel salesman who was concerned about the slaughter of wildlife. As a deputy U.S. Fish and Wildlife Service agent, an honorary position for which he received no pay, he agreed to help Halstead. He was knowledgable about the wholesale fish business, having purchased hundreds of pounds of fish for his restaurant in Piney Point.

The quest had its beginnings with concern raised by state fish and game officials. The Great Lakes, all but written off as dead inland seas by ecologists in the 1960's, were showing significant signs of revitalized life by the mid-1970's—a recovery attributed to stiff water pollution controls. Salmon and trout were stocked in the lakes. The schools of fish prospered. Native warmwater species such as walleyes and yellow perch also showed signs of renewed vigor, increasing in number and invading areas that once were devoid of aquatic life.

But underlying the good news were signs of unrest. Sport fishermen were especially troubled. The recovery was not accompanied by consistent sensational catches. They suspected illegal netters were depleting the schools of fish, and they relayed their suspicions to state fish and game officials. Local authorities also were dismayed by indications that clandestine netters were growing wealthy off their illegal plunder. From all outward appearances, it looked as though a multimillion-dollar outlaw fishery had arisen almost overnight. The state officials expressed their concern to the U.S. Fish and Wildlife Service, and Halstead was ordered to infiltrate the illegal network.

Halstead's initial information came from the intelligence section of the U.S. Fish and Wildlife Law Enforcement Division. Divided into two branches, intelligence consists of undercover and information-gathering sections. Halstead was the division's top undercover agent. The information-gathering branch had pieced together seemingly unrelated bits of information to form a mosaic of slaughter. They had done their work well. From court records and newspaper clippings, from state officials, from anonymous tipsters, from informers, game wardens, and local policemen, intelligence officials gathered sufficient information to point with suspicion at Hoover and Campbell. But the information did not stop there. The intelligence section also had gathered information about the personal habits of the pair.

Hoover managed a bait and tackle shop in a small town not far from Toledo catering to weekend anglers. Campbell's income was more mysterious. He fished commercially. Halstead earlier had made a trip to the area, visiting the hangouts of the pair, talking to their friends. He looked at photos of the two men. He even drank at their favorite tavern, ultimately learning more about the two men than they would ever suspect.

After familiarizing himself, he set up his seafood company, leased a building, and had business cards printed reading:

Piney Point Fish Co.

Piney Point, MD.

Wholesale Fish Suppliers

The phone number on the card was that of a special phone answered by a law enforcement secretary, who covered for Halstead.

His cover established, Halstead made his first contact on April 5, 1977, phoning Hoover at the bait shop, asking for help in obtaining walleyes and yellow perch for his seafood company. Hoover proved to be a reluctant supplier.

"I'm no longer handling commercial fish," he said. "I enjoy sport fishing too much. I can go out and catch fifty, sixty walleyes a day without getting caught."

How about Campbell?

"He's still in the business, as far as I know. He might have some fish, but I can't say for sure."

"Will you ask him?" Halstead asked.

Hoover promised to contact Campbell. When Halstead called again several days later, they agreed to meet on April 27, 1977 at the Toledo Airport.

Campbell selected a popular, expensive restaurant in downtown Toledo for lunch. The maitre d' greeted Campbell and Hoover by name, an act of familiarity that told Halstead that the two ate frequently in the restaurant. It indicated that they must be making good money off their illegal plunder.

Unable to be seated immediately, the four men went downstairs to the bar. Halstead, who holds his liquor very well, ordered a martini. It was a deliberate choice by Halstead. He believed it put suspicious persons at ease; only a dimwit would order a tongue-loosening martini if he had something to hide, something he didn't want to blurt out under the influence of liquor.

In the crowded bar, where conversations could easily be overheard, the talk turned to hunting. Both Campbell and Hoover liked to hunt. Several drinks later, Campbell pulled four photos out of his pocket and showed them to Halstead and Stone. One showed Hoover and Campbell with the spoils of a recent hunt—fifty-two mallards and pintails, a collection of dead ducks far in excess of the legal limit. Another photo showed the pair posing with twenty-three Canada geese, also in excess of the legal limit.

Then Campbell turned over the clinchers. One photo showed walleyes in a net. The fourth showed five large nylon-mesh bags full of walleyes. Each bag contained an estimated 250 pounds of fish.

When they went upstairs to the dining room, the two explained their problem. "We're getting screwed," Hoover said. "We sell our fish in Chicago and New York. They short us on the weight. We'll send them 5,000 pounds of walleyes and they'll say the shipment weighs only 4,500 pounds. And they keep knocking the price down."

"How many pounds of fish can you sell us?" Halstead asked.

"We sell between 75,000 and 100,000 pounds of walleyes each year," he said. "We can't sell you any this year. We've already promised our catch to our regular buyers. Next year will be different. If you pay more, we'll give them to you."

"How much do you want for the fish?" Halstead asked.

"Undressed, $1.29 a pound." Halstead made a quick mental calculation of the total—$129,000. "Can you use that much fish?" Campbell asked.

Halstead did not directly answer. "We'll have to establish our markets. And we'll need the fish processed. We cannot take whole fish. We can only handle fillets. We'll be able to take two- to three-thousand pounds immediately without any trouble, but it might take time to build up our market to where we can sell 100,000 pounds."

Halstead needed time. He hoped the processing request would delay any agreement. He needed the delay for one reason—the U.S. Fish and Wildlife Service had failed to provide him with cash to buy any illegal fish.

"I'll tell you what," Halstead continued. "I'll have a marketing representative from our company contact you. She'll know how we need our fish—what size fillets we can handle, how they should be packaged, when they should be shipped. We can proceed from there."

The luncheon was nearly over. They were all sipping cognac with their coffee. "How do you catch so many fish?" Halstead asked.

"We rig nylon gill nets at night," Hoover said. "They sink below the surface, but we attach small waterproof radio transmitters so we can find them the following night. We always fish with three boats—24-foot Aquasports equipped with big outboards. The fish are put in mesh bags—200 to 250 pounds of fish per bag. That's so if the game wardens surprise us, we can dump them over the side and they'll sink out of sight.

"We fish three boats." Hoover continued. "The fish are only loaded on one boat. We all have Fuzzbusters on the boats to detect the radar from the game wardens who like to sneak around the lake at night without running lights. If we detect radar, all three boats run in circles or figure-eight patterns. Then we all split—each boat heading in a different direction. That way the same warden only has one chance in three of chasing the boat carrying the fish.

"When we come into the harbor, we roll the fish over the side of the boat and wait until the coast is clear. The bags are attached to the boat with lines. We station a lookout two miles down the road from our dock. He alerts us if anything suspicious is happening when we load the fish onto the trucks."

"How do you transport them across state lines to get them to New York and Illinois?" Halstead asked.

"We don't," Hoover said. "The fish are picked up. I'll tell you guys one thing. You cannot use a fish truck with big letters painted on the side saying

'Piney Point Fish Company.' The state boys will stop you every time. You'll need a U-Haul truck or a camper. U-Hauls can go anywhere without attracting attention. But Winnebagos or some camper-like vehicles are better. Nobody looks at those. That's what you'll need to get the fish to Maryland."

Hoover also promised to provide Halstead with false bills of lading. "We get them from Canada, saying the fish originated in Canada. That's the only place you can commercially catch walleyes."

At the end of the lunch, Halstead and Stone promised to return. "We need to set up our market," Halstead said. "Meanwhile, we'll have our marketing representative contact you."

They returned to Washington. To Halstead, it appeared he had a mortal lock on the two outlaw fishermen. They wanted a new market—and he was ready to provide it. He asked Clark Bavin, the chief of the law enforcement division, for funds to buy the fish. Bavin would not give him any money. Without money, Halstead argued, he couldn't buy any fish. Without the fish, he couldn't make an arrest. His pleas fell on deaf ears.

Nor would Bavin ask the state of Ohio to advance the money. Halstead estimated he needed at least $130,000. States frequently provide funds for federal undercover agents, but the amount Halstead needed was too great. Bavin would not budge.

Halstead tried another tactic. He sought from the Interior Department solicitor general permission to re-sell the illegal fish he purchased. He hoped to set up a full-fledged fish wholesale business with Stone's help. The money earned from the sale of the illegal fish would be sufficient to pay for the investigation, he believed.

While waiting for a response from the solicitor general, he returned to Ohio. He brought along Marie Palladini, a diminutive, attractive agent for the Fish and Wildfish Service. She was Piney Point's "marketing expert."

Halstead, Stone and Palladini met with Campbell at the Toledo airport. Accompanying Campbell was a man who operated a hunting club—the club where Campbell and Hoover killed their excessive bags of ducks and geese. They discussed the market. Palladini said she needed specific sizes and weights of the fillets in order to easily market them to restaurants.

"We cannot deliver fish fillets," Campbell said. "We can only deliver them in original form." However, he added that he would help them make contact with local fish processing houses. "Maybe they can clean and fillet and package your fish for you."

Halstead said his company would need to contact the fish processors before he could reach agreement to buy the fish. It was simply another delaying tactic; he still had no money. Halstead promised to get back to Campbell.

When he returned to Washington, the solicitor general issued his opinion. Halstead would not be allowed to re-sell the illegally caught fish. The case was closed.

Fifty tons of illegal walleyes had slipped through Halstead's fingers. For lack of money, he had been stymied. He never contacted Hoover or Campbell again. The big fish had gotten off the hook. Neither man was arrested.

Tennessee Bottomlands

Five-feet ten-inches tall and weighing 220 pounds, Steve Davis presents a formidable physical presence. The hot-tempered Davis had a great deal of fighting ability. One of his more remarkable tavern engagements involved a man who struck Davis on the side of the head with a pool cue. The cue stick broke on impact, stunning Davis only momentarily. The man who wielded the pool cue paid dearly for his misjudgement, crumpling under an angry fusillade of Davis' blows.

Now, Davis was cursing the ice. A mid-December cold front had moved into Tennessee overnight, forming skim ice on Tennessee-Kentucky Lake. Davis was launching his boat in the predawn blackness at a public ramp near his home in Eva, Tennessee. The ice cracked sharply as he pushed the boat off the trailer, but that did not deter Davis, who made a living as a local duck-hunting guide. He had three clients who wanted to gun waterfowl. They were Halstead and two fellow U.S. Fish and Wildlife Service agents— Dave Kirkland and Vern Broyles. Davis did not know the true identities or purpose of his clients' visit.

"This goddam ice is gonna ruin our hunting," Davis declared, speaking to no one in particular. "Son-of-a-bitching ice is gonna chase all the ducks out of here."

Nevertheless, the three agents boarded the boat and scooted out into open water, where Davis pushed the throttle on the outboard to wide-open. The boat skimmed across the black expanse toward the blind—nearly 1½ miles distant.

The date was December 14, 1977. Halstead had flown to Memphis two days earlier, where he met Kirkland and Broyles. The three men had rented a car at the airport and driven to Camden, Tennessee, a few miles from Davis' home.

Halstead's mission was to find, if possible, the person or persons who had stolen a cannon net and four cannons from a nearby goose-banding site on the Tennessee National Wildlife Refuge. Both the Tennessee Fish and Game Department and the U.S. Fish and Wildlife Service were embarrassed by the theft. Also, they feared an unscrupulous poacher might use it to trap wholesale numbers of geese. The net, which measures 60 by 70 feet, is fired from four small cannons over geese feeding on the ground—birds lured to the target area with corn. The net falls harmlessly on the geese, preventing them from taking wing. Biologists use the net to trap birds for banding.

Local authorities had provided Halstead with the names of several persons who might have been responsible for the theft. Among those was Davis, a former employee of the Tennessee Fish and Game Department.

Davis often bragged about his illegal hunting; it was public knowledge in local taverns. He operated in conjunction with Sanford Parks, owner of the Wismer Court and Restaurant in nearby Camden, who provided accommodations for visiting hunters. Parks advertised his motel as "A Sportsman's Paradise."

From his home in Newark, Delaware, Halstead called Parks in November to set up a hunt, saying friends in Memphis had recommended him. Parks took the bait and suggested Halstead book a three-day hunt beginning December 13. Halstead agreed, sending a $100 down payment in the mail the same day. He enclosed a personal check signed with his pseudonym—Robert J. Hall.

Halstead requested that he be accompanied by at least two fellow agents. Davis' reputation as a brawler had preceded Halstead's phone call. A federal agent, in a letter to Halstead, had said Davis "should be considered dangerous." Halstead wanted to take no chances if trouble developed or his identity was exposed. Halstead's superior in Washington agreed to send the additional agents.

When the three agents and Davis reached the duck blind, all were nearly frozen. The damp cold penetrated their heavy down jackets. The north wind was bone-chilling. Davis tied his boat to the back of the blind, where he had constructed a small camouflaged boathouse to hide the craft from the skeptical eyes of wary, circling ducks. The four climbed into the blind and took seats on a wide bench.

The blind, erected on pilings over the water and thatched with cedar boughs, was enormous. Four men could gun with ease. Davis had placed an unusually large spread of decoys in front of the blind. More than 150 mallard decoys, along with a sprinkling of Canada geese decoys, bobbed on the surface of the water.

"Take the plugs out of your guns," Davis ordered. "No goddam game warden is gonna bother us today in this weather."

Plugs are small wooden dowels inserted in a shotgun magazine to prevent it from holding more than three shells. Federal law prohibits gunning waterfowl with a gun capable of firing more than three shots. The restriction is designed to prevent hunters from killing more than their limit and reducing crippling losses of wild birds.

Halstead hesitated after Davis issued his command. "Are you *positive* a game warden won't catch us?" he asked.

"Christ no, it's too cold. They don't want to go out on the water in this crap. And, besides, in this open water we'll be able to see them coming in plenty of time to put the plugs back in our guns."

Halstead unscrewed the magazine cap on his 12-gauge pump shotgun. Kirkland and Broyles followed suit.

Within minutes, a hen mallard flashed across the decoys. Kirkland jumped up to shoot. At the sound of his gun, the duck crumpled and fell to the water. Soon, more ducks crossed the decoys. By daylight, the four had killed two mallards, a black duck and a ring-necked duck.

But then a lull set in. The hunters grew colder. Halstead produced a pint of apricot brandy and unscrewed the cap. Davis' reputation as a drinker prompted Halstead to attempt to gain his confidence by bringing a bottle on the hunt.

"Want a nip to ward off the cold?" he asked Davis as he held out the pint of brandy. Davis quickly took the bottle and tipped the pint to his lips, taking a healthy swallow. He handed the bottle back to Halstead, who raised it to his lips. The pint bottle was then passed down the line to Kirkland and Broyles. Several nips later, the apricot brandy produced the expected effect. Davis began talking nonstop, a diatribe directed at Willie J. Parker, the U.S. Fish and Wildlife Service agent who commanded federal agents stationed in Tennessee.

"That goddam Parker. He's got two or three helicopters, boats, fast cars and everything else. And what does he do? He just catches the poor hunters of Tennessee. He doesn't do a goddam thing about the rich hunters."

Davis talked about his arrest the previous year by Parker. He was charged with possessing untagged ducks, a minor violation. "I killed 149 ducks that day. Everything was frozen over except small pockets of open water on the Tennessee River. That goddam Parker only found a few—and then he couldn't prove I shot them. He could only get me for untagged ducks."

Halstead was growing steadily angrier. Parker was an enormously successful agent. His patrols routinely nabbed numerous poachers.

"Parker can't be that bad," Halstead asserted. He wanted the conversation to end. He was afraid he or Kirkland or Broyles might accidentally say something that would tip off Davis that the three knew Parker, something as minor as calling Parker by his first name.

A few more ducks flew into the decoys. The four men fired. But the gunning was poor. "Christ, you guys want some great shooting," Davis said, "you ought to come down here in late August or early September. We kill wood ducks by the bushel. We dump corn or milo and kill fifty to seventy-five goddam woodies in an afternoon shoot. Jesus, it's fast shooting."

"Is it *that* good?" Halstead asked.

"You better believe it," Davis replied.

Three Canada geese then swerved toward the decoys. All three fell dead to the water under a fusillade of shots. Davis lost his anger. He became ecstatic. "We don't kill hardly any geese out of this blind," he said.

Halstead suggested they call it quits for the day. "It's too damn cold. The ducks aren't moving. And we're out of brandy." His suggestion was greeted with affirmative responses. They got back in the boat and headed for shore.

The next day, the four gunned only a short while, killing one duck. The ice conditions were getting worse. Halstead cancelled the third day's hunt.

Broyles and Kirkland returned in January, gunning the Camden Bottoms, a state-controlled hunting area. They shot from a tree line bordering a flooded milo field frozen by sub-zero temperatures. The gunning was poor.

After the hunt, they went to a commercial picker, who for a fee cleaned and plucked hunter's birds. Davis got twenty-four frozen ducks and three freshly killed geese from the picker and gave them to the agents to take home. He refused to accept money for the birds, allowing them only to pay the picker for the chore of cleaning the birds.

Davis said he shot the geese the evening before.

In September, Kirkland and Broyles returned for the fabled wood duck shoot. The gunning season for wood ducks had not yet opened, but the trio killed nearly fifteen wood ducks while gunning on Bird Song Creek.

The wood duck shoot marked the end of the undercover operation. Davis was charged with gunning during the closed season and shooting over the legal limit and fined $200 in U.S. District Court. He also faced several state charges. Parks, who arranged Davis' hunts, was charged with aiding and abetting. He was fined $250.

As for the cannon net, it was never found.

Tigers and Leopards

Not all of Halstead's investigations were conducted in marshes, creek beds, or in the woods. This time, he found himself walking across the thick pile carpet of a posh gift shop in downtown Washington, D.C. A discreet chime had signaled his entrance into the small exclusive store, and the sight of the merchandise was breathtaking. There were tapestries from the Far East, fourteenth century Chinese antiques, rare ivory and jade treasures from India, sapphire jewelry from Sri Lanka, antique china from England and objets d'art from Czarist Russia.

The object of Halstead's investigation was a tiger pelt. Several days earlier a friend of a fellow agent reported the shop was offering a tiger pelt for sale. Tigers are classified as an endangered species, which makes it illegal to sell the pelts in the United States. Violators face a maximum sentence of one year in jail and a $10,000 fine.

Halstead's mission, however, involved more than simply confirming whether the store was offering a tiger pelt for sale. He wanted to find out, if possible, who sold the tiger pelt to the store. And how did they obtain the contraband hide?

After pausing to survey the expensive merchandise, Halstead found no tiger rug on display. But he was soon approached by the store manager, a well-dressed man with a suave, polished manner who shall be called William Stanley, asking if he could help.

"I'm looking for a tiger skin rug for my wife," Halstead said. "A friend of mine told me you had one for sale."

"I'm sorry," Stanley replied. "We have no tiger rugs for sale. However, we soon will have a leopard rug. Its price will be $1,000."

Leopards, native to Asia and Africa, also were listed as endangered at the time and were illegal to sell. Perhaps, Halstead thought, the tipster had mistakenly identified the pelt.

"Why is the leopard so expensive?" Halstead asked.

"It's quite difficult to obtain tiger or leopard skins because of the endangered species laws," the store manager explained. "Not just anyone can bring a pelt into this country."

The leopard skin, he explained, had been brought into the United States by an employee of the International Development Bank. Persons who work for such organizations are given a certain amount of diplomatic courtesy by U.S. Customs officials, who sometimes decline to search their luggage.

"Could I see the leopard?" Halstead asked. "My wife has her heart set on a tiger or leopard rug for our den."

"I wish I could show it to you," Stanley replied. "Unfortunately, it's in storage." But he promised to let Halstead inspect the pelt in a couple of days. The two men exchanged business cards. Halstead's read: Delaware Down and Feather Co., Newark, Delaware. Robert J. Hall, Representative.

On the surface, the probe seemed to be developing routinely. Halstead thought he might buy the leopard pelt on his next visit, which would enable him to bring charges against the store manager. But the remark about the person who brought the rug into the United States and his connection with the international diplomatic community intrigued Halstead. There were implications that this case was bigger than he thought.

Three days later, he returned to the shop. Stanley was not there but Halstead was directed to a nearby office. When he entered, he found Stanley seated at a conference table with three men and a woman. Stanley immediately recognized Halstead. "This is the gentleman I was telling you about," he said to the others. "The one who is interested in the leopard rug."

Introductions were made, and a man introduced as Francis Hoffer, the president of the corporation that owned the gift shop, indicated the rug was not for sale.

"Let's show it to him anyway," Stanley said. "At least he'll know what to expect if he wants to buy another one." Hoffer said he would get it and left the room. Halstead and Stanley went into an adjacent office to wait. In the course of the conversation, the two men discovered they shared a passion for hunting. Stanley spoke of African safaris, Indian shikars, and big-game hunting in the United States. Halstead had never hunted in Africa or India, but he had done quite a bit of hunting in the West. His comments seemed to spark Stanley's interest.

"We rent pieces of land in Wyoming for elk and deer hunting," he said. "We entertain a lot of diplomats who like to get away from Washington and do a little hunting."

Hoffer then returned, saying he could not find the key to the storeroom. Stanley apologized for being unable to show Halstead the leopard, and for the fact it was no longer for sale, but he promised to find Halstead another rug. And as he walked Halstead to the door, he said, "I just thought of something. We'll soon be importing some zebra and Moroccan sheep skins. Do you think you'd be interested in anything like that?" Halstead was non-committal, but he promised to keep it in mind.

A few weeks later he received a phone call from a man who spoke with a clipped British accent. He asked for Bob Hall.

"This is Hall," Halstead replied.

"My name is Myles Peel. Francis Hoffer told me you want to buy the leopard-skin rug at the shop."

"That's right," Halstead told Peel. "But Hoffer said it wasn't for sale."

"He was mistaken," Peel said. "I believe he may have had another skin in mind—one that was promised to someone else. This one was killed by a friend of mine on a ranch in Central Africa, and I can let you have it for $1,000."

"If it's a good one, I'll take it," Halstead said. "But I want to see it first."

"I can see no problem with that. My friend also has another leopard hide. If you want it, or if you know someone who does, let me know. I'm going to Africa this summer and can pick it up then."

The two agreed to meet in two weeks in Washington so that Halstead could inspect the leopard skin. At the appointed time, he met with Peel in a hotel bar. After a drink, they went to a nearby apartment. It was expensively furnished with the same kind of antiques and objets d'art sold in the gift shop. Peel showed Halstead the leopard pelt. He ran his fingers through the thick fur. Its soft gold and its black rosettes glowed luxuriantly in the late afternoon light.

"I'll sell you this hide and the other one I mentioned for $1,700," Peel told him.

Halstead agreed to buy both. He wrote out a check for $600, promising to pay the remainder when the second hide was delivered. Peel told Halstead he could pick up the first hide at the gift shop, which he did several days later.

With the leopard pelt in his possession, Halstead wrote a memo to his superiors, requesting them to alert the U.S. Customs Service that Peel would be returning to the United States through John F. Kennedy International Airport in New York in July. He asked that authorities search Peel's luggage for the second leopard skin. Under no circumstances, Halstead said, should his undercover role be disclosed.

The month of July passed. Halstead heard nothing. Then he received a phone call from Peel.

"I've been advised not to transact further business with you," Peel said coldly. He added that the $600 Halstead had paid for the leopard pelt in his possession was sufficient payment. Peel offered no explanation but from the tone of his voice Halstead felt Peel knew he was a lawman. No charges were brought against Peel.

The incident gnawed at Halstead. Why had Peel bothered to tell him he would have nothing further to do with him? Ordinarily, persons selling contraband disappear if they learn they have sold illegal goods to an undercover agent. Had Peel been trying to send Halstead a message? Was he trying to tell him to forget any further investigation, that more influential individuals than Halstead were involved? And how had his identity been discovered? Had he been betrayed by someone in his own agency or in the U.S. Customs Service?

His cover had been blown, he was sure, at least as far as Peel was concerned. Now that he had penetrated a smuggling operation involving endangered species, he wasn't certain what his next step should be.

Two weeks later, his problem was solved. A tipster informed U.S. Fish and Wildlife authorities that leopard and tiger pelts were being sold at an import shop located in the same complex as the gift shop. It was operated by a man named A.S. Kahn.

With Faye Ruddy, a young agent posing as his daughter, Halstead once again drove to Washington. When they arrived Halstead discovered the store was the same one he had visited previously, now apparently under new management and a new name. A tiger pelt was displayed against a wall, its legs outstretched.

With Kahn at their side, Halstead and Ruddy examined the tiger pelt, rubbing their hands across the thick orange and black striped fur. Kahn said he also had a leopard skin in the store's back room.

"Aren't these illegal?" Halstead asked.

"There's no problem with these hides," Kahn replied, adding that they had been brought into the United States by an Asian diplomat. He brought out the leopard hide, and both agents examined it. Not wanting to appear over-anxious, Halstead thanked Kahn and said he would think about it. Two weeks later, Halstead and Ruddy returned.

"My daughter wants both the tiger and leopard skins," Halstead said. "How much will they cost?"

"The tiger is $3,950," Kahn said. "The leopard goes for $950."

"That's kind of high, isn't it?"

Kahn paused briefly, apparently assessing Halstead. "I'll tell you what, I might take $4,500 for both."

"You've got a deal," Halstead said. He was taking no chances this time. He wanted the pelts in his possession. But Kahn was cautious. He said he would have to check with his "banker" before selling the pelts.

A few days later, Kahn called Halstead in Delaware to say the $4,500 asking price was acceptable. They agreed to meet for lunch to complete the sale the next day at a restaurant between Washington and Newark. When Kahn arrived, Halstead, Ruddy, and Cindy Delaney, another wildlife agent, were seated at a table in the dining room. Two other agents, Larry Thurman and Leo Badger, were sitting at a nearby table.

Kahn was talkative over lunch. He dropped the names of two ambassadors and said the daughter of a U.S. consul worked in his store. Halstead speculated that he had stumbled onto an international smuggling ring composed of people with diplomatic immunity who brought contraband and items on which high duties were imposed into the various countries where they were stationed—items like jewelry, rare art objects, and pelts of endangered species. He suspected these were sold through a network of stores in cities like Washington and Moscow (as Stanley had indicated), and probably other international capitals such as London, Paris, Calcutta, and Hong Kong.

After lunch, Halstead gave Kahn a check for $4,500, hoping he would not demand cash and cause a further delay. They walked out to the parking lot to transfer the goods. When Kahn opened the trunk of his car and handed Halstead the box containing the tiger and leopard pelts, agents Thurman and Badger moved in.

"You're under arrest," Thurman said, handcuffing Kahn. They also handcuffed Halstead to prevent Kahn from suspecting he was working undercover. Halstead wanted to keep his role secret for future investigations.

Kahn was charged with violating the Endangered Species Act and was fined $500. No charges were ever brought against Hoffer or Peel.

South of the Border

John Prentice, not his real name, was a hunting guide, who liked to tell his clients about the time he was apprehended by Mexican authorities and taken into custody at Matamoros, across the border from Brownsville, Texas. He was being interrogated when he asked to go to the bathroom. There, he bribed two guards, giving them $500 in American currency. In a flash, the heavy-set Prentice made his break, running out of the restroom, down a flight of stairs, and onto the street. He kept running toward the International Bridge despite the shots fired by the bribed guards, who aimed high to avoid hitting the fleeing, well-heeled gringo. Prentice was out of breath and panting, his sides ached from the strain, when he finally crossed the border into American territory. But he had outwitted the Mexicans. He was safe.

Prentice seemed to enjoy outwitting the Mexicans. From his office he operated a guide service, offering to take American hunters across the border to shoot waterfowl and doves. Prentice's operation was not unique—several other Americans along the Mexican border also arranged hunting trips to Mexico. Legions of hunters booked trips with these outfits.

The allure of hunting in Mexico is quite easy to understand. Game is plentiful—and the law is often ignored. Hunters who have crossed the Rio Grande speak openly of daily kills exceeding one hundred birds apiece—and these are the comments of hunters who are not extraordinary shots or exceptionally skilled huntsmen. They are run-of-the-mill gunners who find that in Mexico they often can kill more birds in one day than they can in an entire hunting season in the United States.

The wide-open gunning was overlooked by Mexican officials until 1976, when Mario Casillio was named minister for wildlife and parks. He had heard of Prentice's operation; indeed, Casillio ran two hunting camps himself for visiting Americans. He knew of Prentice's escape and asked for help from Keith Parcher, a U.S. Fish and Wildlife Service agent who speaks fluent Spanish. Casillio wanted to arrest Prentice.

As a result, Halstead found himself, in February 1976, sitting in Prentice's office discussing hunting. "We shouldn't have any trouble getting lots of birds tomorrow," Prentice was assuring Halstead. "Doves are darkening the skies. The shooting should be real good."

Several weeks earlier, Halstead had called Prentice from his office in Delaware. Posing as Robert J. Hall, he inquired about booking a hunt. "Shouldn't be any problem," Prentice drawled. "All we have to do is arrange a time when you can hunt and when I'm not booked up." A three-day hunt, he added, would cost $489.

The two arranged a date and Halstead immediately mailed a check for $109 as a down payment.

With his ruddy complexion and graying hair, Prentice radiated confidence as the two sat in his office. "We got the shootin' if you got the shoulder," he drawled. "Lots of our hunters go back home with shoulders that are black and blue from shootin' so much." Halstead chuckled at Prentice's statement. It was the sort of comment visiting hunters loved to hear, he thought.

Prentice then drove Halstead to a nearby motel, parting with the comment, "I'll see you at 5 a.m."

Casillio's major problem in arresting Prentice was learning the outfitter's whereabouts and when he would cross the border into Mexico, where Casillio had arrest powers. Part of Casillio's problem in learning the operations of Prentice stemmed from local officials in Reynosa and Brownsville. Prentice paid immigration officials $7 for each American he brought across the border, Halstead learned. He also paid the chief game warden $20 for each hunter, a sum designed to insure there would be no interference for game law violations, Halstead was told. The local Mexicans were loath to give up these payments. They wanted them to continue. They were not about to tell Casillio when Prentice crossed the border. Halstead's hunt was different, however. Parcher notified Casillio when the hunt was scheduled. And from his motel room that evening, Halstead called Parcher to inform him of his exact departure time. Casillio would be ready, Parcher said.

Wardens pose with illegal bag of loons killed before gunning was halted on Cape Lookout, North Carolina. Halstead is third from right, standing.

Henry Cofer, the waterfowl biologist who tipped Halstead about the theft of ducks from waterfowl traps on Assawoman Wildlife Management area in Delaware, holds a banded black duck.

Halstead on board a government boat that patrolled
Alaskan coastal waters in search of salmon poachers.

Halstead, right, and agent Dave Kirkland pose with a day's kill of waterfowl
on the Tennessee-Kentucky Lake.

An Indian bonnet made from illegally purchased eagle feathers.

Desert bighorn ram shot by Halstead's
guide in Southern California.

Wheelbarrow full of dead ducks shot on Tangier Island.

Faye Ruddy, Halstead's fellow undercover agent, holds a bag of illegally shot ducks taken at Pruitt's Tangier Island gunning camp.

The following morning, Prentice arrived on schedule. Halstead put his gear in Prentice's pick-up truck and the two drove to a nearby pancake house for breakfast, where they met Prentice's cook and guide, Juan.

With Juan following in his auto, the two crossed the border at Reynosa. The crossing posed no problem—Prentice handed the immigration officer a white envelope and was whisked through.

"Do you have to pay each time?" Halstead asked.

Prentice nodded his head in affirmation.

The two headed south into the flat farmlands of northern Mexico, croplands tended by toiling peasants. They had driven perhaps 15 miles when two autos with flashing red lights pulled alongside, the occupants motioning Prentice to pull over. When the motorcade stopped, four armed Mexicans quickly jumped out of the two autos and ran to the pick-up.

"Out! Out!" they shouted.

When Halstead and Prentice stepped out of the cab, they were told to put up their hands. Both were frisked. When they discovered neither was armed, one swarthy guard looked menacingly at Prentice. "Go ahead and run this time," he taunted, a reference to Prentice's earlier dash to freedom. He remained as motionless as a marble statue.

The raiding party was headed by Casillio, who had flown in from Mexico City. Casillio never gave any hint that he knew Halstead's identity.

Both men were hand-cuffed and taken to the federal building in Matamoros, where they were held in a detention facility. Prentice almost immediately gave Halstead a wad of bills and some checks.

"I doubt they hold you," he whispered. "Deposit these in my bank account, and call my wife and my secretary. Have them contact my Mexican lawyer."

Halstead was taken to a small room.

"Why did you enter Mexico illegally?" asked one officer.

"I didn't enter illegally," Halstead replied. "I came across with Prentice. He said everything was legal." Halstead spoke no Spanish. His inquisitors spoke little English. In the detention center the heat was unbearable and the smell was worse. His time in the detention center was broken only by occasional questioning.

Halstead had been in custody less than three hours when he noticed a guard wearing Prentice's new shoes. What, he thought, would they take from me?

Halstead steadfastly refused to give a statement that he had violated

Mexican law. The Mexican authorities even produced a nine-page type-written statement in Spanish, asking him to sign the "confession." Halstead refused.

The original plan, worked out between Casillio and Parcher, called for Halstead to be immediately released. But a snag had developed. Immigration officials were irate over Casillio's arrest of Prentice. They wanted to continue receiving their "white envelopes." Casillio had no authority over immigration officials; his department controlled wildlife and parks. Only his status as a big honcho in Mexico City kept the local immigration authorities from acting hastily.

Halstead knew nothing about the bad blood developing between Casillio and the immigration officials. Casillio spent most of his time that day talking long-distance to high government officials in Mexico City, seeking to convince them to issue orders to free Halstead.

Halstead was released after nearly ten hours, and immediately crossed the border into Brownsville. He then returned to Delaware. Within several days, Halstead later heard, Prentice was released on bail and returned to Texas.

Halstead thought his involvement was a bit strange. Being ordered to book a hunt so that an official of a neighboring country could arrest an American was unusual, to say the least. Perhaps, Halstead thought, the arrest would benefit wildlife if Casillio cracked down on the corrupt game warden in Mexico.

The following autumn Halstead booked another hunt in Mexico with an outfitter located in southern Texas. The cost for this week's hunt was $2,150. Prentice was nowhere to be seen.

In the morning, Halstead and the other hunters were picked up by assistants of the same Mexican game warden whom Prentice had paid $20 a day. In the pick-up truck a blender had been installed to enable the hunters to make margaritas during the ride to the gunning sites. The assistant game wardens escorted the American hunters across the border to insure no problems developed.

Halstead was gunning with two sporting goods dealers from Kansas. They told Halstead they once shot 103 white-fronted geese in one day's gunning in Mexico. They laughed at Halstead for bringing only one shotgun.

"You need two shotguns," they told him.

The three hunters were taken into the countryside for a dove shoot. Halstead and his two companions hid in a hedgerow beside a milo field.

Enormous flocks of white-wing and mourning doves flew overhead. Halstead shot until his gun barrel was so hot he no longer could hold the gun. Even trying to miss, he shot forty-seven doves. A Mexican boy retrieved the birds that fell into the field.

The Kansas hunters shot more doves. Each had a Mexican field hand to load their shotguns. They would shoot, hand the empty gun to the Mexican, and receive a fully-loaded firearm in return. By alternating the guns, they also eliminated the problem of over-heating. They each shot nearly 150 white-winged and mourning doves before the gunning ended.

When they returned to Texas, each hunter carried only 25 doves—the maximum permitted by U.S. law. The remainder were left in Mexico.

Halstead became despondent. He felt he had been used. The decision to have him book a hunt with Prentice in order to enable Mexican authorities to arrest the outfitter had been a waste of time, he felt. The corrupt Mexican game warden was still in business. The Mexican government could not—or would not—halt the corruption in its own ranks. And Americans were still pouring across the border to participate in the slaughter.

Our National Emblem

The handsome cardboard sign posted in the door window of Ashland Indian Supply read "Back in 15 Minutes." Halstead decided to wait. He had driven to Ashland, Montana, with his wife in hopes of purchasing illegal Indian artifacts—headdresses, war bonnets made with feathers from illegally killed bald and golden eagles, eagle-talon necklaces and eagle-bone whistles.

Halstead was unsure what he might purchase from Carl Leynard, proprietor of Ashland Indian Supply. An FBI informant earlier had told the FBI field office in Portland, Oregon, about a widespread black market for illegally killed eagles. The FBI report was forwarded to Halstead. In addition, the Montana Department of Fish and Game gave Halstead the names of six persons who were believed to be dealing in the outlawed eagle trade.

Halstead selected Leynard as his first target for two reasons. First, Leynard lived near the North Cheyenne Indian Reservation. Indians are a good source for dead eagles. Frequently, the Indian women themselves will transform a dead eagle into a war bonnet in the time-honored tradition of their ancestors, complete with rawhide, buckskin, colorful beads and long plumes of eagle feathers. These headdresses are avidly sought by collectors of Indian memorabilia. Second, Ashland is located in southeast Montana, the state's prime bobcat trapping range. Trappers use dead rabbits to bait their bobcat sets. Eagles are attracted to the rabbits like ants to a picnic luncheon and scores of eagles die each year in bobcat traps. Many of these are sold illegally to supply the black market eagle trade.

Halstead's car, parked in front of Leynard's store, was a typical government-issue pale green sedan totally lacking any decorative chrome. To disguise it, he had mounted on the front doors two plastic signs—the kind often used by real estate salesmen. The red, white and blue plastic signs, attached to the doors with magnets, read: "Delaware Down and Feather Co., Newark, Del." His pseudonym was, as usual, Bob Hall. His business card stated he was proprietor of the feather company.

Within minutes, Leynard returned. He got out of his car, addressed them warmly with a "howdy," and invited them inside his store. It featured a wide-ranging display of Indian goods—shawls, blankets, fringe beads, necklaces, beaded belts, bells, feathers, Indian records, buckskin jackets, and turquoise. Hanging on the wall behind the cashier's counter were the objects of Halstead's search—two eagle-feather bonnets.

While Halstead's wife, Evelyn, browsed through the store, Halstead handed Leynard his business card.

creates illusion of ← Supply & DEMAND!

"I don't want to buy any feathers at this time. I sell wholesale. I need bonnets and bustles," Halstead said, pointing to the bonnets on display.

Leynard, a slightly-built man of average height with ruddy, sandy hair, eyed Halstead keenly. "Those aren't for sale," he said, "They're over 100 years old. However," he added, "I'm having three new bonnets made. They should be ready in a few days."

Watch for creating a market to fill a transitional void.

Halstead made a quick mental calculation. A simple bonnet takes approximately 100 eagle tail feathers. An eagle has twelve tail feathers. Since one or two generally are broken in transit, a simple bonnet requires 10 dead eagles. A war bonnet with a long trail requires the tail feathers from approximately twenty eagles. The cost ranges from $350 for a simple bonnet to $11,000 for a full medicine man costume with a double trail bonnet and extensive beadwork. Raw eagles—dead birds whose skins have been salted to preserve them—sell for $100. The economic incentive was more than sufficient to stimulate a black market.

Halstead decided not to press for the purchase of the three bonnets being made. He wanted to give the impression he had more than one source of eagle bonnets for his feather company, that he had been in the illegal business for some time. "I'll get back to you," he said.

His wife, meanwhile, selected some Indian trinkets and a buckskin jacket. Halstead paid nearly $55 for the items. Three weeks later, on June 18, 1973, he called Leynard from Delaware to ask if the bonnets were ready.

"No, the three aren't finished yet," he said. "But I have another bonnet and a bustle that I can sell you."

"How much do you want for them?"

"I can't give you a price right now. I don't know what my cost will be until they are delivered."

"Can you get them by late next week? I should be in Montana then."

Leynard said delivery should be no problem. Halstead promised to visit Ashland. On the 29th, he entered Leynard's store.

"Howdy," said Leynard, who was sitting behind his desk. When Halstead walked up to the counter, Leynard pointed to a war bonnet and bustle hanging on the wall next to his desk. "There they are," he said.

Halstead examined both to make sure the ceremonial Indian wear contained only genuine golden eagle feathers. He did not want dyed turkey feathers substituted. Both the bonnet and bustle were genuine. "How much are you asking for them?" he asked.

"Three hundred and fifty dollars each."

Halstead made out a check, and they carried the bonnet and bustle out to Halstead's car in the parking lot beside the road. "Aren't you worried about the game warden driving by and seeing you with eagle feathers?" he asked.

"It's no problem," replied Leynard. "We have only one game warden and he rarely comes by."

"Can you get raw materials for me?" Halstead asked. "I can use three sets of wings and two tails."

"I'll try," Leynard replied. "I'll call you when I get them."

The eagle probe had its beginnings three years earlier. Postal employees objected to the stench of packages delivered to a man who lived in Grand Rapids, Michigan. The complaint prompted federal authorities to investigate, and he was found to be the recipient of rotting eagle skins and feathers. His arrest in 1970 resulted in the seizure of a quantity of eagle feathers. His files and correspondence disclosed what appeared to be a nationwide ring of persons who trafficked not only in eagle carcasses, feathers, talons and bones, but also the finished products—war bonnets, bustles, lances tipped with eagle feathers, eagle-bone whistles, necklaces made from eagle talons, kachina dolls decorated with eagle feathers, peyote fans.

Letters found in Grand Rapids—from Indians, trappers, cattlemen and weekend hunters—prompted U.S. Fish and Wildlife Service agents William Fuchs and Richard Branzell to believe a full-scale investigation should be undertaken. Bald eagles had been protected since 1940 when Congress passed the Bald Eagle Protection Act. Subsequent amendments to the law extended this protection to golden eagles.

Both Fuchs and Branzell had noted the extensive collections of eagle merchandise offered for sale at Indian pow-wows in the Middle West and by individual hobbyists. They wrote their supervisor, Doug Swanson, in Minneapolis, who in turn requested that Washington begin a full-scale investigation. More than two years elapsed before Washington finally decided to launch a nationwide eagle probe. Halstead, the bureau's most effective undercover agent, was ordered to spearhead the investigation.

His probe began with the assistance of an official of the Boy Scouts of America. The official often helped eagle scouts purchase a genuine eagle feather as a memento of their rank. The official knew it was illegal for the young scouts to buy eagle feathers and he agreed to become an informant.

The chance union of Halstead and the boy scout leader proved very fortuitous. Halstead proved an apt student. He learned what Indian artifacts were most sought-after, what articles were genuine, what prices were paid for raw eagles, tail feathers, and finished products. He learned to tell a genuine eagle feather from a dyed turkey feather. (Take the feather in your hand. Hold the lower stem and quickly jerk your hand with a strong sweeping motion so the feather feels a rush of air. A turkey feather will buckle; its spine is too weak to withstand the strain. The strong spine of a genuine eagle feather will not bend.)

Halstead's first foray took him to upstate New York to the Tuscarora Indian Reservation and across the border into Canada, where he made his first two purchases. The date was June 1972. From that time, Halstead gradually worked his way westward. Most sellers gave him the name of others who engaged in the outlaw trade. He moved from New York to Pennsylvania to Ohio, Michigan, and Wisconsin. From there he traveled to Minnesota, South Dakota, Nebraska, and North Dakota. He found eagles and eagle products offered for sale virtually everywhere—in private homes, at roadside curio shops, at famous tourist sites such as the Wisconsin Dells, on Indian reservations such as Wounded Knee and Pine Ridge. His accumulated evidence was growing.

By the time he stopped at Ashland Indian Supply he was probably the foremost purchaser of eagle feathers in the nation. Shortly before purchasing the bonnet and bustle from Leynard, an Idaho man offered to sell Halstead ninety-seven eagles at $100 apiece.

Halstead was becoming so successful he began restricting his purchases to avoid establishing a major new outlet for the eagle peddlers. He bought only a few items from each dealer—enough to assure the probability of a court conviction—before moving to another supplier. And the black marketeers were helpful; once he made a purchase, they often recommended several other individuals who might have eagle feathers or products for sale.

Halstead's probe came at the same time the nation issued an alarm about disappearing eagles. Most environmentalists blamed the pesticide DDT for the declining eagle populations, believing the pesticide forced the birds to lay eggs with shells so thin they broke during incubation. Halstead did not accept the theory that reproductive failures caused the sharp drop in the eagle population.

"Guns and traps are doing in most of the eagles, not pesticides, as is commonly believed," he asserted in memos to Washington.

Halstead returned several times in 1973 to Leynard's store. When Leynard was unable to supply the items Halstead wanted, he referred him to other dealers. Halstead found himself moving even farther westward—to Kooskia and Blackfoot, Idaho, Lodge Grass, Montana, Pendleton and Portland, Oregon.

Once, Halstead was busy on another investigation when Leynard called. He sent Dave Kirkland, another U.S. Fish and Wildlife Service agent, who said he was Halstead's partner. Leynard sold Kirkland three sets of wings and one set of tail feathers.

The last purchase was made in May, 1974. Halstead and Kirkland picked up four raw eagle carcasses for $320—a low price because the feet were missing on one of the birds.

By now, Leynard felt confident in Halstead's company. He invited Halstead and Kirkland into his office one day for coffee. "Most of my eagles are caught during the winter by trappers," he told them. "I salt them down to preserve them. I get from twenty-five to fifty eagles each winter." He announced his plans to build a small shed behind his store to keep the birds.

"They get to smelling bad," he complained.

Leynard employed several Indian women to produce his artifacts in a back room of his store. The women made everything from war bonnets to bead necklaces.

Halstead visited Leynard only once more. In early December, he stopped with another agent to talk business. The purpose was not to buy eagles. It was to identify Leynard to the other agent who planned to arrest Leynard.

On December 5, 1974, the raid took place. U.S. Fish and Wildlife Service agents and U.S. Marshals fanned out across thirteen states to arrest the individuals who had sold eagles and eagle products to Halstead. Nearly seventy-five persons were swept up as a result of the probe, which lasted over a three-year period. For his sales, Leynard was fined $150.

Politics in Wildlife

For several years Halstead had heard rumors about the gunning on Jack Dukes' farm near Taylors Bridge, Delaware. The shooting invariably was extraordinary, informants said, with most hunters taking home full limits of Canada geese. This was remarkable since the geese were attracted to two small ponds near Dukes' farmhouse, sites that normally would be shunned by the wary Canadas. Moreover, Dukes was a well-known conservationist in the state. He was an official with Delaware Wildlands, an organization devoted to preserving wild habitat, and had been chairman of an organization that opposed the proposed construction of an oil refinery on the coast in New Castle County.

But the rumors persisted. Finally, just before Halstead left for California to pursue developments in a desert sheep poaching case, Dave Kirkland, Halstead's assistant, asked to look into the matter.

"Go ahead," Halstead replied. "See if you can find anything."

Several days later, Kirkland and Jeff Blakemore, another agent, flew over Dukes' farm. They saw what appeared to them to be an unusually large number of geese feeding in a very small area on one of the ponds. There also were geese present that appeared to be live decoys.

The next evening the two agents entered the farm on foot under cover of darkness. As they approached the pond, nearly fifty wild Canada geese took wing. Seventeen stayed behind. These birds, they discovered, were unable to fly; their wings had been pinioned. They took mud samples from the bottom of the pond, but discovered no corn.

The following day they repeated the procedure, finding nearly 600 wild birds mingling with the pinioned geese. Again, they found no corn on the bottom, yet their instincts told them something was wrong. Geese would not be attracted to the pond in such great numbers without an adequate supply of food.

The fourth day Blakemore began an all-day stakeout. He walked onto the property before dawn, found a hiding place in the brush and waited. Around 10 a.m. the geese began flying over. The pinioned birds called incessantly to their wild, free-flying brethren and the wild birds tumbled down to the pond. Blakemore watched as they concentrated near one corner of the pond to compete for food. The location was only 25 feet away from a goose-hunting pit. In mid-afternoon, the geese began leaving.

By 3:30 p.m., the wild geese had departed, leaving only the pinioned geese in the water. Blakemore watched a man dressed in blue coveralls and wearing hip boots step out of the farm house and walk to a nearby barn. Soon he was driving a tractor towing a trailer toward the pond. The man, who agents later identified as Dukes, drove to the southwest corner of the pond, got off his tractor and waded into the water. He retrieved a sunken metal washtub and returned to the barn. The following afternoon, Kirkland and Blakemore watched as Dukes retrieved another empty sunken metal tub from the pond's bottom. This time he replaced it with a tub filled with whole kernel corn. It was located in the same area where the geese had been concentrated. Kirkland collected a sample of the corn for evidence.

The same procedure was repeated the following night. Dukes replaced an empty washtub with one filled with corn. More kernels were collected for evidence.

The tub ploy is often used by poachers. Its purpose is to confine the corn. Often, when corn is scattered by hand, some floats away or is not eaten by the wildfowl. Game wardens find the uneaten corn and charge the hunter with shooting over bait, a federal offense. The tub is designed to insure that no loose grains escape to be found by an alert game warden.

Kirkland returned to the farm three times the following week, twice finding Dukes replacing the empty tubs with ones filled with corn. On the third morning, the pinioned geese were not on the pond. They were locked in the barn. Neither was the empty tub on the bottom of the pond. Kirkland retreated a mile away to await developments. At 7:30 a.m. he watched a flock of geese descend to the pond. Guns boomed. Kirkland got in his auto and drove to the farm. As he entered the lane, he watched three more geese set down. Guns again boomed. Two geese fell to the water with a splash. Dukes waded out to retrieve the birds.

When he returned to his blind, Kirkland was waiting. He charged Dukes and six other hunters with gunning with the aid of live decoys and shooting over a baited area. The latter charge against Dukes was eventually dropped.

Federal law prohibits hunters from using tame or semi-domestic water-fowl as decoys on the grounds that it enables the hunters to take unfair advantage of wild waterfowl. In addition, the law prohibits hunters from putting out grain to attract birds because it causes wild waterfowl to lose their sense of caution.

On the surface, the Dukes episode was another routine case. But Halstead returned from California to find himself facing a political firestorm.

One of those apprehended with Dukes was the son of a prominent National Wildlife Federation official. Letters and phone calls were made to politicians and high-ranking bureaucrats in Washington. The prostesters' message was unanimous: Halstead and Kirkland had to go. Halstead was blamed because he was the agent-in-charge of Delaware, and he had allowed Kirkland to arrest the goose-hunting party.

Spencer Smith, director of the U.S. Fish and Wildlife Service, reacted to the political pressures quickly. Halstead was ordered transferred to Washington, D.C. Smith described it as a promotion for Halstead despite the fact that Halstead faced a $3,000 cut in pay and a higher cost of living. Kirkland was ordered to New York City. He also was told to turn in his government vehicle. (Other agents routinely transferred to New York City are allowed to keep their autos.)

Halstead was furious as was Kirkland. He had backed Kirkland—and now he was the victim of a political lynching. He refused to acknowledge the transfer. He refused to report to Washington. Instead, he called J. Caleb Boggs, a U.S. Senator from Delaware. Boggs was a long-time personal friend and backer of conservation causes.

"Senator, I need help," Halstead began.

Boggs listened sympathetically. When Halstead finished, Boggs said, "I'll do everything I can."

Boggs was not simply another senator. His efforts for conservation had won him the admiration of many within the Department of Interior. His support in Congress was essential for many U.S. Fish and Wildlife Service programs. Under normal circumstances, a senator's interest would be re-flected with a phone call from an aide to the service director or the congressional liaison aide. In rare instances, the director might be asked to speak with the senator—in the senator's office, of course. Most senators, grandiose poseurs that they are, refuse to visit the office of a bureaucrat. It would be demeaning to their station in life.

But Boggs was no average senator. He stalked into Smith's office and demanded to know what the hell was going on and put Smith on the spot.

Halstead was summoned to Washington the next day for a showdown meeting with Smith, deputy director Vic Schmidt and Chuck Lawrence, head of the enforcement division.

The deputy chief was especially put out by Boggs' visit. "Why is a U.S. senator walking into this office?" he demanded to know.

Halstead did not bother to respond.

"We're giving you a promotion. Transfers are a part of life when you work for the federal government. Why won't you come to Washington?" he continued, neglecting to mention that the so-called "promotion" would force Halstead to take a $3,000 annual pay cut and live in a city with a higher cost-of-living.

"You've become useless in Delaware," he added, forgetting that in the two previous years Halstead had been awarded merit raises and superior performance citations for his work in Delaware.

Halstead let Schmidt rage. He would burn himself out soon, he knew, and the negotiating could begin.

Finally, Halstead was offered a compromise plan. If he would file a formal complaint alleging that Kirkland did not follow orders, Halstead could remain as the chief federal agent in Delaware. Halstead refused.

"Kirkland did what I would have done—if I had been there. I gave him permission. He acted properly."

Halstead's refusal infuriated Smith and Schmidt. They were caught in the middle. They could attempt to fire Halstead and Kirkland, and earn the enmity of Boggs, which they did not want. But, if they let them remain in Delaware, several other protesting congressmen would be offended.

Chuck Lawrence, the head of law enforcement, backed Halstead and Kirkland.

In the end, a compromise was reached. Halstead would remain in Delaware, but would be assigned full-time to undercover operations—one of the first agents ever assigned to full-time undercover work. He would report to the Washington office. He would not make patrols in Delaware. Kirkland would be transferred to Denver and would be allowed to keep his auto.

The compromise, everyone involved immediately recognized, had nothing to do with more effective protection of the nation's wildlife. It was a purely political decision.

Dukes, the prominent conservationist, appeared in court later to answer to the charges. He pleaded guilty to gunning with the aid of live decoys and was fined $35. The baiting charge was dropped.

The Trophy Hunters

Halstead stared out of the window into blackness. The Continental Air Lines jet in which he was riding winged across the skies high over the Rocky Mountains. Night had fallen. No lights could be seen below in the rugged, sparsely settled terrain. No winking lights to signal reassurances of civilization. Nothing but black emptiness.

Halstead was en route to California on a mission so secret that fewer than five persons knew his assumed identity—or his purpose. In the footwell beneath his seat, he guarded a small camera bag filled with assorted items a typical middle-aged hunter might carry—camera, film, field glasses, matches, compass, aspirin, Preparation H. Buried at the bottom of the bag, seemingly lost in the clutter, Halstead had hidden a small radio transmitter and $2,500 in twenty-dollar bills, the serial numbers of which had been recorded.

The flight marked Halstead's first penetration into the rarified world of big-game poaching, a secretive society of wealthy "sportsmen" and unscrupulous guides. Their goal in life is to kill big-game animals with huge antlers, horns, tusks or skulls. They want an animal whose physical dimensions are so extraordinary that the name of the hunter who shot the "trophy" will be published in "North American Big Game," the record book of big-game hunters.

The book is published by the Boone and Crockett Club, an organization founded by Theodore Roosevelt. The club began its record-keeping in 1932 in an effort to provide hunters with a means of comparing their kills with those of other hunters.

Halstead hoped to kill a desert bighorn sheep, the most prestigious big-game animal on the North American continent. The desert bighorn, native to the parched mountains and high plateaus of the Southwest, is the rarest sheep on the continent. Once plentiful, the bighorn populations plummetted with the advance of civilization. Domestic sheep introduced in the West by early settlers infected the herds with lungworm, a parasite which killed thousands of the animals. Feral burros also invaded sheep ranges, competing for sparse vegetation and water. The result was disastrous for the species. Altough thousands of hunters apply for special desert sheep hunting permits each year, fewer than thirty rams are permitted to be legally killed.

Halstead's infiltration into big-game poaching rested with California outfitter Gary Swanson. Two months earlier, Halstead had phoned Swanson to set up a hunt for desert bighorn ram. And now, as the jetliner swept westward, Halstead sipped a martini and stared out the window, mentally reviewing the details of his cover story to protect his true identity and the events that were bringing him across the continent.

The investigation began in April 1970 when the California Department of Fish and Game received an anonymous letter declaring that Swanson conducted illegal desert sheep hunts in Southern California, where the species had been protected since 1873, and in Mexico, where sheep hunting is sharply restricted.

Swanson, a prominent taxidermist, painter, and hunting guide from Yucaipa, was well-known to state officials. An influential member of the Society for the Conservation of Bighorn Sheep, an organization dedicated to reversing the downward trends of sheep populations, Swanson often testified before state legislative committees, urging more funds be spent to save the rare desert bighorn. He helped build artificial waterholes in the arid Jacumba Mountains to provide life-giving water to parched sheep. He conducted surveys for the Fish and Game Department, noting sheep population trends and charting seasonal movements. Swanson was, in fact, one of the most knowledgeable desert sheep authorities in California. State officials conducted a cursory investigation, but found nothing amiss.

One month later, a man who harbored a personal grudge against Swanson contacted Keith Parcher, a U.S. Fish and Wildlife Service agent then stationed in Sacramento. The informant described Swanson's operation with astonishing detail, prompting Parcher to start his own probe.

The superficial inquiry, conducted with utmost discretion to avoid alerting Swanson, confirmed the allegation that the Yucaipa taxidermist was spearheading a large-scale poaching ring. Halstead was ordered to infiltrate the ring.

At the time, Halstead was living in Newark. He enlisted the aid of Louis Edgell, a personal friend, to establish a cover. Edgell, president of the Edgell Construction Co., a highway construction firm in Dover, Delaware, gave Halstead permission to pose as the company's public relations executive. He instructed his secretary to accept all calls for Halstead, to act as if the agent was indeed a member of the firm. He tutored Halstead on the details of highway construction to complete his cover story. He explained the firm's equipment and the highway builders' language. Halstead learned about the spread of equipment—the fleet of scrapers, pushers, rollers and compactors. He learned the techniques—the clearing and grubbing, the cuts and fills, the sub-base and base. Halstead studied erosion controls, side slopes, guard rails and culverts.

To establish Halstead's bonafides as a big-game hunter, Larry Wills, a U.S. Fish and Wildlife Service agent based in Seattle, Washington, convinced Bert Klineburger of Jonas Brothers, one of the world's largest taxidermy firms, to write a letter to Swanson, naming Halstead as a man who would soon make contact. Klineburger once employed Swanson in his Seattle taxidermy shop. He said that Halstead was a man who could be trusted, who desperately wanted a full-curl desert bighorn to hang on the wall of his trophy room.

In July, Edgell's secretary placed the initial person-to-person call to Swanson's home. After the outfitter answered, Halstead took the phone, identified himself and began talking.

"Mr. Klineburger tells me you're the best sheep guide in the United States."

Swanson reacted cautiously. He ignored the topic of sheep hunting.

"What's Klineburger's first name?" he demanded.

"Bert," Halstead replied. "He sent a letter of introduction to you—at least he said he did."

"Wait until I get on a private phone before we discuss sheep hunting." When Swanson came back on the line, he asked, "What can I do for you?"

"I want to kill a desert sheep and check out your operations."

Halstead explained that he was a public relations executive for Edgell Construction, that he and the company president frequently took clients on hunting trips. "We're looking for good outfitters," Halstead said. "If I get a ram and find you run a good operation, we'll want to book more hunts."

Swanson listened silently. When Halstead finished, the outfitter replied, "I can get you a ram. It will cost $3,000 for a five-day hunt."

Halstead balked. "That's pretty steep. Edgell doesn't want to pay that much money."

Swanson paused. "Would you agree to $2,500?"

Halstead accepted. They selected the date of September 13 to begin the hunt.

"Bring lightweight clothes. It's damn hot in the mountains—rugged country," Swanson advised. "Also, don't bother bringing a rifle. We'll provide one." As for payment, Swanson said, "I don't accept checks. I want cash, preferably tens or twenties, I don't like fifty- or hundred-dollar bills."

Halstead promised to make flight reservations and call back to confirm his plans. Ten days later he again spoke with Swanson to outline his flight plans to the airport at Ontario, California.

"That's good," Swanson replied. "I'll meet you at the airport."

In August, Swanson called Halstead. "Can you change your hunt to September third?" he asked. "I've got two other hunters already scheduled on the thirteenth. I've got the goddamdest trophy ram in the world spotted, but it's in extremely rough country. The other two hunters aren't in good enough shape to climb the mountains where it lives."

Halstead agreed to the revised plans.

His airplane landed at the Ontario airport shortly after midnight on the second of September. Halstead, wearing a brown pin-striped suit, was greeted in the terminal by Swanson, a rugged, handsome 29-year-old man who stood 6 feet, 4 inches tall and weighed 220 pounds. Accompanying Swanson was Ray Pocta, a Yaqui Indian and carpenter who worked part-time as a guide for Swanson.

After picking up his luggage in the baggage claim area, the trio got into Pocta's camper-equipped pick-up truck and drove to Swanson's house. "I won't be able to guide you," Swanson announced. "I've got another client to pick up. Pocta will take you out. I'll see you in the afternoon."

Swanson gave Halstead a quick tour of his sprawling stone-and-mortar ranch house, including the trophy room. Halstead looked with envy at the desert sheep mounted on the wall. Four heads consisted of horns and skulls. Another was a fully mounted head with large, curving horns. Halstead hoped to linger and engage in conversation, perhaps learning the origin of the sheep heads. But Swanson was impatient.

"We've got to hurry. You've got to drive all night," he said.

Halstead handed Swanson a packet of marked twenty-dollar bills whose serial numbers had been recorded. He promised to pay the remaining $1,000 on completion of the hunt. Swanson agreed, then suggested Halstead quickly change into his hunting clothes. "You can leave your suit in my closet," he added.

Halstead picked up his suitcase in one hand and his camera bag in the other to go into the bathroom to change. Swanson immediately reacted.

"Why are you carrying that?" he barked, pointing a finger at the camera case with the hidden transmitter.

Halstead looked him in the eye. "I carry my green cabbage in this bag," he replied, indicating that he meant his cash. Moments earlier, he had withdrawn the packet of twenties from the case.

The look of suspicion drained quickly from Swanson's face. He laughed. "In that case, you better hold onto it," he said.

Pocta and Halstead began the long drive south. Shortly after three a.m., Pocta pulled his pick-up over to the side of the road. "I'm nearly dead from a hunt," he said. "I need some sleep." He turned off the engine, leaned against the door and quickly fell asleep.

Halstead could not sleep. His nervousness increased as he sat in silence beside the sleeping Pocta. The quiet was broken by a sudden thunderstorm. Heavy rains pelted the cab of the pick-up. Thunderclaps rumbled across the night skies. Forks of lightning slashed down from the heavens. Still, Pocta did not awaken. At four-thirty, Halstead could contain himself no longer.

"Hey," he said, shaking Pocta. "How about I drive while you sleep?"

Pocta agreed and they exchanged places.

"Just follow this road," Pocta said and then he fell back to sleep.

The motion of the pick-up soon wakened Pocta, who sat in silence while Halstead drove.

"Why aren't we hunting around Ontario? Swanson said that's where the big sheep lived," Halstead asked.

"All the big heads in the area have been taken," Pocta replied.

They drove southward past Palm Springs, past the Salton Sea. As the sun peeked over the mountains at dawn, they drove through Jacumba, finally turning off the highway onto a dirt road. Pocta resumed driving as they climbed the mountains and by eight, they were at the end of a remote mountain road. Pocta parked the pick-up behind huge boulders, where it was hidden from view below.

Halstead stepped out of the cab and looked at a dry and barren landscape of incredible harshness. The dun-colored, boulder-strewn Jacumba mountains supported only sparse, withered vegetation. The arid mountains stretched to the horizon, a bleak and lonely land where sidewinder rattlesnakes and desert bighorns struggle to survive. The morning temperature already was over 100 degrees.

Pocta pulled out a .308 Remington rifle hidden under a sleeping bag in the camper. He handed it to Halstead, briefly instructing him how the bolt-action rifle worked. He gave Halstead four cartridges and a small rucksack containing the day's provisions—a can of Spam, a loaf of bread and a gallon of water.

The pair set off on a northeasterly course, traversing a sharp, rocky ridge before descending into a deep ravine where there was a small spring Pocta said often attracted sheep. They found no sheep near the spring. They climbed the rocky side of another mountain. On the other side, Pocta said, two springs were located.

The rugged climbing tired Halstead. The searing sun caused him to perspire heavily. He gasped for breath in the thin, hot air. When they reached the top of the mountains, Halstead was near total exhaustion. He had gone nearly thirty hours without sleep. The effort to climb the rugged peak took its toll.

"I've got to go back to the truck," he said. "I can't take any more of this."

"Do you want me to go on?" Pocta asked, a polite way of asking if Halstead wanted him to shoot a ram, a not uncommon practice afield.

"Yes," Halstead replied.

He handed Pocta the rifle. The guide moved on, disappearing over a distant ridge. Halstead slowly worked his way back to the pick-up, a journey that lasted two hours.

He heard two shots. One report echoed across the mountains shortly after Halstead parted company with Pocta at noon. The other came around three in the afternoon as he rested by the pick-up truck. Halstead looked around, but still could see no sign of Pocta. He sat back and listened to the moan of the wind, the only sound in the mountains.

His reverie was interrupted suddenly when he heard the growl of a pick-up truck. He turned to see Swanson bring Jim Bensley, an employee in his taxidermy shop, and a paint contractor from New York City, who also wanted to kill a desert bighorn. Swanson chatted briefly before driving northward.

Halstead waited nearly three hours more. He snapped photos of the area. He hid his radio transmitter in a rock crevice, a move designed to enable him later to accurately determine his location. About six, the weary Pocta returned. In his rucksack he carried a ram's head and neck. Blood from the freshly slaughtered sheep dripped from the pack.

"I saw eight ewes and one half-curl ram, then I heard this noise in a cave where a spring is located. There were two rams fighting. They charged past me about 15 feet away. I picked the biggest one and this is it."

Pocta collapsed on the ground. He was exhausted from lack of sleep, from packing out the ram, and from climbing the steep mountains.

Swanson returned thirty minutes later. His new client, the paint contractor from New York, said he had seen a good ram but could not get a good shot.

Halstead's sheep head was skinned, put into a heavy plastic garbage bag, and placed in the back of Swanson's pick-up truck. Swanson, Halstead and Jim Bensley began the long drive back to Redlands, carefully taking a back route to avoid the Border Patrol, which Swanson said often stopped vehicles to look for illegal aliens. Pocta stayed behind with the hunter from New York.

Halstead was dropped off at a local motel about two a.m., where he paid Swanson the remaining $1,000.

At nine a.m., Swanson returned, bringing Halstead's suit and dress shoes. Swanson was accompanied by his wife, his two children and a woman who worked in Swanson's taxidermy shop.

Swanson's mood was jubilant that morning as they stopped at a nearby restaurant for breakfast. He was planning a hunt for Marco Polo sheep in Mongolia later that year, and the discussion centered around sheep hunting.

"Do you want to kill a grand slam?" Swanson asked. A grand slam is the goal of all dedicated sheep hunters. It consists of killing all four species of wild sheep native to North America—the Dall, stone, Rocky Mountain bighorn, and desert bighorn. Very few hunters have achieved a grand slam.

"I'd like to—if I could work things out," Halstead replied.

Hunting permits for stone and Dall sheep, which inhabit Canada and Alaska, are relatively easy to acquire. Rocky Mountain bighorns are relatively rare, and hunting permits are difficult to obtain.

Swanson suggested Halstead book a hunt with two brothers he knew in Wyoming. The price would be about the same as his desert sheep hunt, Swanson said. The outfitter promised to vouch for Halstead.

Soon afterward Halstead said good-bye. Swanson's employee drove him to the airport at Ontario. He gave her a $10 tip, thanked her for the ride, and disappeared into the terminal. The hunt was over . . . almost.

The next day Halstead and Parcher, the agent in Sacramento, flew over the area Halstead had hunted and found three other sheep hunting parties. None were part of Swanson's operation.

Three weeks later, on the basis of Halstead's testimony, federal and state authorities acquired a search warrant and raided Swanson's home and taxidermy studio, seizing all records, correspondence, sheep heads, skulls, and hides. Swanson was not in the country at the time of the raid. He was hunting Marco Polo sheep in Mongolia.

The records provided agents with innumerable leads. They fanned out across twenty-one states to track down the hunters who had gunned sheep with Swanson. It was the most widespread big-game poaching investigation ever conducted.

Federal charges eventually were brought against thirty-three sheep hunters. Nearly all pleaded guilty and paid $500 fines.

Many hunters escaped prosecution. Authorities estimated nearly 150 sheep were killed by Swanson and his clients from 1964 to 1970, grossing Swanson nearly $400,000, agents estimated. Records disclosed, and guides confirmed, that one of Swanson's clients was the brother of the Shah of Iran.

A Vermont hunter who pleaded guilty to killing a desert bighorn cooperated with authorities and booked a Rocky Mountain bighorn sheep hunt the following year with the Montana outfitter Swanson had recommended to Halstead. Accompanied by another undercover federal agent, the pair shot a Rocky Mountain bighorn *inside* the boundaries of Yellowstone National Park. They also killed two elk inside the Crow Indian Reservation.

On the federal charges, Swanson was fined $500 and placed on probation for six months. Pocta and Bensley were fined $250 each and placed on six-months probation. All three also pleaded guilty to state charges.

Swanson moved to Arizona and became a successful wildlife artist. In 1977, he was invited to participate in Wyoming's celebrity One-Shot Antelope Hunt, a widely-publicized affair featuring politicians, actors, industrialists, and other prominent personalities. Swanson was the second hunter to kill an antelope that year, dropping his pronghorn with one shot.

In 1980, the Foundation for North American Wild Sheep issued its first "Wild Sheep Conservation Stamp." The stamps are sold to raise money for conservation projects to save wild sheep. The stamp features a miniature reproduction of a ruggedly handsome painting of Rocky Mountain bighorn sheep. The artist's signature on the painting was familiar to Halstead. It is signed: Gary R. Swanson.

Salmon of the Columbia

Posing as Rex Huggins, a representative of the S. D. Seafood Co., Halstead wrote a letter inquiring about the availability and price of salmon. He followed his letter with a phone call a week later. And now he was about to land at the airport in Portland, Oregon, for a face-to-face meeting with Mary G. Settler, proprietress of a salmon wholesale house.

Mrs. Settler was something of an enigma to law enforcement officials. She operated on both sides of the Columbia River, and Washington and Oregon authorities believed she was dealing in illegal salmon. She had been arrested previously on minor charges involving illegal fish, but authorities believed something greater was involved—and asked the federal government for assistance.

At the same time, Mrs. Settler was unquestionably an extraordinarily shrewd and successful businesswoman. She had begun her career as a fish cutter in a local fish processing house, but she was not content to spend her life working for someone else. She saved her money, studied the operation and learned the tricks of the trade—a remarkable feat considering the cutthroat competition of the wholesale fish business. She soon owned her own fish processing plant, one of the largest wholesalers of salmon in the Pacific Northwest. Mrs. Settler, in fact, represented a classic American success story.

Her rise to prominence followed the decline of salmon populations in the Columbia River. While no one accused her of being solely responsible for the vanishing spawning runs of salmon, it was thought she was taking an extraordinary number of salmon and selling them for a tidy profit.

The widespread poaching of salmon posed a stumbling block to fish and game officials in Oregon and Washington, who imposed severe restrictions on salmon fishermen in hopes of reversing the downward trend of salmon runs. The restrictions, however, had failed to halt the decline in the salmon population.

Mrs. Settler, a well-dressed, slightly plump woman with black hair, was on hand to greet Halstead when he got off the plane at Portland. She was accompanied by her husband.

The three ate lunch in downtown Portland, while Mrs. Settler gently probed Halstead's reason for wanting to buy salmon.

"We want to expand our market on the East Coast, and salmon is a fish we figure many restaurants will buy," Halstead replied.

The S.D. Seafood Company, Halstead continued, hoped to offer a greater variety of fish than the usual seafood house. Consumers were demanding different kinds of fish from restaurants, he added. They were getting tired of the traditional striped bass, bluefish, flounder, shad roe, crab and lobster dishes found on most seafood menus in the mid-Atlantic states. Afterwards, Mrs. Settler drove them to her processing plant on the Columbia River. During the drive along the rolling hillsides flanking the river, she continued her interrogation of Halstead, giving the agent a glimpse into her operations.

"How much salmon do you want to buy?" she asked.

"We figure we'll need about 200 pounds a week," Halstead replied.

Mrs. Settler laughed. "We don't sell less than 20,000 pounds at a time," she said. "Nearly all my salmon goes to a broker in San Francisco. I prefer to do business that way." She revealed that a large quantity of her salmon is frozen and stored in Seattle, and sold in small quantities throughout the year. "I spent $74,000 last year just to freeze and store my salmon," she said. The freezing of the salmon proved to be a wise marketing decision. During the spawning runs, when salmon are plentiful, the prices drop. Prices rise when the fish become scarce. By selling frozen salmon, she was able to maximize her profit.

Her largest shipment that year, she added, totalled 165,000 pounds. "It was sold to the Japanese," she said.

Halstead was astounded. Clearly, the woman had no problem securing large numbers of salmon despite the doomsayers' warning that the runs of salmon in the Columbia River were disappearing.

When they reached her processing plant, Halstead noted five trucks parked outside the building. Two were refrigerated trucks. Two trucks were flatbeds with insulated sides and top. On entering the plant, Halstead noticed several Indians hanging nets in a loft. Attached to the nets were black corks and black buoys. Most fishermen use brilliant colors for their buoys in order to be able to easily spot them. Black buoys are used for illegal night fishing. "All my fishermen are aware they are under surveillance," she said. "Both Washington and Oregon game wardens are trying to catch them."

On the main floor, amidst the cleaning tables, women and men quickly dressed the evening's catch of chinook and sockeye salmon. Most of her salmon were chinook, the largest and most valuable of the Columbia River salmon.

Halstead spent the night at a nearby hotel. The following day, Mrs. Settler offered to sell him 2,400 pounds of sockeye or red salmon for $2.80 a pound. She also said she would sell him sturgeon at any time of the year for 90 cents a pound.

Halstead promised to get back in touch quickly, and left that same day for Washington. He pleaded with his superiors to give him the money to buy the salmon, but he was not given a penny, even though the cost for 2,400 pounds of salmon amounted to only $6,720.

Several days later, Halstead called Mrs. Settler. "I've talked it over with my boss," he said, "and we agreed we cannot handle that amount of salmon. The market simply isn't big enough."

Halstead then issued a written report, giving details of everything he learned during his undercover probe. The report was turned over to authorities in Washington and Oregon.

Acting on Halstead's information, Oregon authorities inspected a shipment of fish at the Portland Airport, a shipment destined for San Francisco. It contained illegal salmon. Mrs. Settler was convicted on sixteen felony counts and sentenced to five years in prison.

Isle of Infamy

Halstead stood on the county dock at Crisfield, Maryland, a small fishing community on the lower eastern shore of the Chesapeake Bay, waiting for the ferry to take him to Tangier Island. His duffel and cased shotgun were piled beside him on the wooden dock. The goose hunting season opened the next day, and Halstead said he hoped to gun some of the Canadian honkers. To the curious, Halstead added that he was a retired real estate speculator. As for his purpose, "I want to get away from the world, to have a good time and to hunt."

As a means of underscoring his concern for tranquility, he was accompanied by a woman he said was his secretary. She looked like a tourist—or a clandestine girlfriend who knew little about gunning. Her name was Faye Ruddy and she, too, was a U.S. Fish and Wildlife Service agent.

Several weeks earlier, traveling under the pseudonym of Robert J. Hall, Halstead had made his first trip to Tangier, a small island located in the middle of the Chesapeake Bay, to check out the facilities of Pruitt's Paradise Inc., a commercial duck-shooting camp. He was intrigued by what he saw.

Now, under the warm October sunshine and with the Virginia gunning season about to get underway, Halstead was ready to return. His wait on the dock was not long.

The Mate, the 43-foot ferry which operates between the mainland and the island, soon came into view and pulled alongside the dock. Halstead stepped aboard, stowing his duffel and that of Faye Ruddy. The lines were cast off and the boat slowly disappeared from view as it twisted along the serpentine channel leading to the windswept, open waters of Tangier Sound.

83

Halstead's initial assignment was to confirm or disprove allegations contained in two letters sent to the Washington, D.C., office of the U.S. Fish and Wildlife Service. Written by out-of-state hunters, both letters alleged that hunters at the camp openly defied the law, an attitude they said was encouraged by the guides. Gunners regularly killed scores of ducks each day, far in excess of the legal limit, they asserted. On good gunning days, when scudding clouds and strong northwest winds forced the ducks to fly to sheltered waters where the gunners lurked, the toll of dead game was awesome. Guides stuffed ducks into gunny sacks to make it easier to carry the birds, they added.

Halstead's first inkling that the conscience-stricken, letter-writing hunters were correct occurred when he stepped off the ferry. A guide picked up their duffel and took them to the camp, a short distance away. "Bring along plenty of shells tomorrow and take the plug out of your gun," he said. "Don't worry about the law. They can't touch us. Shoot all you want."

The reference to the so-called "plug" is well-known to duck hunters. Federal law prohibits waterfowl hunters from shooting a shotgun capable of holding more than three shells. Most repeating shotguns are capable of carrying five or six shells. A wooden dowel or "plug," inserted into the magazine when the arm is disassembled, reduces the number of shells the shotgun can hold to three. The gun then is in compliance with federal law. Outlaw hunters frequently remove the plug, enabling them to unleash a deadlier five- or six-shot salvo and increase their kill.

Halstead knew that Tangier Island had posed a problem for years for law enforcement agents. Separated from the mainland by fourteen nautical miles of water, the island seemingly was immune from a surprise raid. Local residents could see strange boats approaching long before they reached the island, broadcasting warnings over their citizen's band radios to hunters and guides in the marshes. The warnings gave outlaw hunters time to dispose of illegally killed ducks. Most guides carried a gunny sack and a brick. In the event a warden came by, the dead ducks would be stuffed into the gunny sack containing the brick and dropped overboard. The bag would sink, hiding the evidence.

Halstead and Ruddy were taken to Pruitt's hunting camp. The camp, such as it was, consisted of several house trailers which provided sleeping accommodations and a dining room for visiting hunters. Women slept in a separate trailer with the cooks and domestic help. After unpacking his clothes, Halstead complied with his guide's suggestion and took the plug out of his 12-gauge pump gun.

Ruddy watched curiously as Halstead reassembled his shotgun, the blue steel glistening under the trailer lights. "How many do you think you'll kill tomorrow?" she asked.

"Lord knows," he replied.

Before dawn the next morning, Halstead was awakened by his guide knocking on the trailer door. "Time to get up," he yelled. "The birds will be flying in less than an hour."

Halstead dressed quickly and walked over to the dining room for breakfast. Ruddy stayed behind in camp. Halstead told everyone his "secretary" was not a hunter. In reality, her job was to prowl the camp, talking to the help to learn more about the operation.

When the first faint wash of pink shone on the eastern horizon, Halstead was motoring north in a 16-foot aluminum boat to Tangier's famed shooting grounds—the marshy shoal extending northward from the island for miles. His guide, Glen Autry, already had constructed a brush blind, a low structure which camouflaged his small craft.

They quickly tossed the decoys overboard on reaching the blind. The plastic imitations of floating ducks bobbed lifelike on the water as they pulled their boat behind the blind.

"Load up," the guide said. "The ducks should be knocking our hats off any minute."

Indeed, the first flight of ducks soon swept across the decoys with a flash. They circled widely and came around again for a landing. When they set their wings, Autry shouted, "Let's take 'em!"

Halstead threw his shotgun to his shoulder, tracked a gliding duck and squeezed the trigger. The bird crumpled and fell to the water with a splash. Halstead fired again at another speeding duck; he missed. Quickly, he touched off three more shots, crippling one bird. Autry, meanwhile, had dropped two birds. In less than five minutes, the pair had killed three ducks and crippled one, which escaped.

For the remainder of the day, Halstead discovered that ducks were the primary targets. Only geese were legal to shoot but the duck-gunning season would not begin for several weeks. But guns roared whenever ducks approached the decoys.

At the end of the day, Halstead and his guide had killed only five ducks and one Canada goose. The shooting had been slow due to the mild weather. The big northern flights had not yet arrived on the Chesapeake wintering grounds. But the gunning provided Halstead with sufficient detail about Pruitt's operation.

"The letter-writers are correct," he told Ruddy on his return to camp.

Halstead forwarded his information to Washington three days later. His memo stated that lawlessness prevailed at Pruitt's Paradise, that hunters at the camp primarily shot ducks and paid no attention to the game laws. He was ordered to return to the island and to continue his "informational" investigation. He made several more trips, forwarding his findings each time to Washington. But he heard nothing more. It was almost as if his reports had been misplaced or forgotten; Tangier disappeared into an investigative limbo.

Unknown to Halstead, a bureaucratic dispute was taking place over who would have jurisdiction over the probe, a squabble which left the law enforcement division impotent and meanwhile, nothing was being done to stop the slaughter of ducks that season.

The only law enforcement incident occurred after the season ended that year. Pruitt and two of his guides were arrested several days after the season closed when federal agent Darcy Davenport surprised the trio by sweeping in on a float plane and landing in front of their blind. Pruitt was charged with gunning during the closed season and was fined $250 and placed on two years probation with the stipulation that he not hunt during the probationary period. But within 30 days, the sentence was reduced, the probation was lifted, and the fine slashed to $50.

The following autumn, Halstead was ordered back to the club, this time to gather evidence which could stand up in court. Halstead balked at the assignment. He didn't want to gun on the island. It was too close to Virginia Beach, where he was raised and many gunners who visited the island came from the Norfolk-Virginia Beach area. He feared a hunter might recognize him and blow his cover. He transmitted his fears to Washington, but he was overruled.

When he returned to the camp to begin the new 1975 gunning season, he was once again accompanied by Ruddy. (Higher-ups in the division had decided that a man and woman traveling together would be less suspicious as undercover agents.) Halstead hunted at the camp eight different days that year. Four other federal undercover agents—Vern Broyles, Marsha Kronan, Mary Monaghan and Joe Hopkins—also traveled to the island under the guise of hunters.

Halstead established a routine of gunning in the morning and resting in camp in the afternoon. His evenings were spent talking with guides and visiting hunters.

"The conversation is always the same," he told his superiors. "Everybody wants to know how many redheads you killed." Redheads were the primary species killed at the camp. The shooting of redheads was prohibited by law that year because of the species' perilously low population. But this did not deter the hunters.

"Two men from Pennsylvania killed seventy-two redheads in one day's gunning. The toll was kept down because the men ran out of ammunition by three p.m.," Halstead reported. Another time he witnessed "five bushels of redheads being thrown overboard to float away with the tide because the hunters would not take them home." On good gunning days, when the wind blew and the restless ducks took wing, the camp's game house would be full of ducks. "I've seen more than 200 on the floor of the game house at one time," he said.

The birds brought back to camp were so-called "good ducks." Hunters killing less desirable species such as goldeneyes, old squaws, buffleheads or mergansers didn't bother retrieving them. The ducks were left in the water to drift away with the currents to the empty expanse of the Chesapeake Bay.

But the lawbreakers did not confine their activities to simply shooting more than the law allowed, gunning protected species or hunting during the closed season. They staked out tame Canada geese as live decoys, Judas birds which would call their wild brethren down within shotgun range. Many out-of-state hunters even refused to buy a Virginia hunting license. If the gunning was slow, the hunters and guides would stay out past sunset, the legal quitting time for waterfowl hunting.

Once Halstead participated in a night shoot. He left camp at sunset, motoring with his guide into the marshes to a site where fowl frequently passed in flight. When the birds winged past, they shot them, aiming at the birds silhouetted against a silver moon. Halstead shot Canada geese, brant and redheads.

"I don't believe that anyone hunting in the Pruitt operation can legally hunt," he wrote in a memo to Washington.

The club, incorporated in 1969, was founded by Kenneth R. Pruitt Sr., a Tangier native, and ten prominent attorneys and businessmen from Norfolk and Virginia Beach. Each member put up $1,000 to pay for the purchase of an acre of land on the island and several house trailers, which were shipped over to provide sleeping and dining accommodations. With the exception of Pruitt, none of the club members derived any money from the operation, it was later learned. Instead, there was an understanding that Pruitt would run the club and the mainlanders would get hunting privileges.

Contributing to the wholesale lawlessness was the club's location. Tangier natives are an independent people who fiercely resist progress. They ask for nothing more than to be left alone in a harsh and raw environment, struggling to earn a living by harvesting crabs, fish and wildfowl. Their cloistered life has survived since the island was settled in the 1700s. To most islanders, breaking a game law is not a breach with society; it is a means of rejecting the modern world and preserving the past, when game laws were unknown. It provides a sense of community for the islanders, reinforcing their belief in a way of life that disappeared long ago.

"They're good people," Halstead once said. "But getting them to obey the game laws is not as simple as asking them to clean up their act. It's asking them to change their way of life."

By the close of the season, Halstead had killed fifty-eight ducks and seven Atlantic brant, a small sea goose. The numbers of birds he had to kill disturbed Halstead. He often deliberately shot to miss to keep his bag down. But he knew if he missed nearly every shot, his guide would become suspicious. His kill was mounting, but his Washington superiors did nothing to stop the slaughter. On January 12, 1976, Halstead shot twenty-nine redheads, his largest daily bag.

"I could have killed in excess of a hundred ducks," he reported, but he deliberately jammed his gun and returned to camp for repairs. This was the same day the two Pennsylvania hunters shot seventy-two redheads. It was a banner day for duck shooting—high winds accompanying an advancing storm kept the ducks flying into hunters' decoy rigs all day long.

With each trip to the island, Halstead became more apprehensive. He felt his luck was running out. Guides often spoke during the cocktail hour of how an "agent wouldn't get off this island alive." He once arrived at the island just one day after a boyhood friend from Virginia Beach departed from his hunt. Another time, a visiting hunter who had drank copious quantities of liquor during the cocktail hour looked the soft-spoken, white-haired Halstead in the eye and declared, "You're either an agent or a minister." Halstead laughed at the assertion. Fortunately, the other hunters in the room, who also were drinking heavily, ignored the remark. Halstead breathed an inaudible sigh of relief.

Halstead carried a small radio transmitter hidden in his hunting coat as a precaution. It broadcast his conversation to fellow agents on a boat lying offshore, agents who were prepared to rush ashore and rescue Halstead if his identity was discovered. Ironically, the small radio almost exposed him. A U.S. Navy dentist admired Halstead's hunting coat and tried it on for size. He felt the weight of the transmitter sewn into the lining.

"What's this weight in here?" he asked.

"That's the batteries for my handwarmer," Halstead snapped, hastily grabbing the coat away from the dentist.

Three days after the second hunting season ended, Halstead once again was gunning the island, sitting in a duck blind on the Tangier marshes. Ducks were flying in endless streams in the face of an advancing nor'wester. The date was January 17, 1976. Guns were booming as the birds tolled readily into the decoys.

Halstead waited. He knew his mission was almost over. And then it appeared—the biggest armada ever mounted by the U.S. Fish and Wildlife Service descended on the island. Eight boats, racing through pounding seas, swept down on the marshes. A helicopter, its noisy death-rattle shattering the sound of shrieking winds, dropped out of the sky and landed on the club property. A twin-engine aircraft swooped down on the island airstrip.

"Jesus Christ, let's get to the creek. They're gonna invade us!" screamed Glen Autry, Halstead's guide.

Hunters in the marshes scattered, hoping to avoid arrest by sneaking undetected through the serpentine creeks in the marsh. Their ultimate goal was Smith Island, located about 10 miles north of Tangier. But many found themselves being hotly pursued by a task force of federal agents who defied the 6-foot seas and freezing spray to invade the poachers' domain.

Thirteen hunters and guides were apprehended that day. Follow-up investigations set in motion court proceedings that ended with ten guides, thirty-three hunters, the captain of the ferry boat, *The Mate*, and Pruitt either being found guilty or pleading guilty to assorted charges.

Among those who hunted on the island were two hunters who had held office as Virginia state chairman of Ducks Unlimited, a nationwide organization whose purpose is the perpetuation of wild waterfowl. Indeed, Pruitt himself had contributed substantially to Ducks Unlimited and proudly displayed on the wall of his hunting camp a DU sponsor's plaque.

Pruitt, who faced eighty-three charges, was found guilty on four felony counts of selling migratory game birds—ducks that had been served as meals at the camp. He was the only corporate member of the camp who was charged and he was placed on two years probation.

Halstead estimated 11,000 ducks, mostly protected redheads, were killed on the island during his two-year investigation. If the service had acted after his initial visit, he later siad, the senseless slaughter could have been prevented.

The Collector

To say that the man who shall be called Harry Brant possessed a large collection of stuffed animals would be an understatement. Brant's house was a menagerie of fur and feathers. Halstead never had seen so many mounted heads, animal rugs, and full-bodied mounts in a private dwelling. As he walked through Brant's house, snarling jaguars, tigers, leopards, and bears, whose pelts and heads had been transformed into rugs, stared up at Halstead from the floor. Elk, moose, deer, sheep and antelope stared down at him from the walls. Stuffed owls, ducks and hawks perched forlornly on tables and mantels. A pair of mounted African crowned cranes stood in a corner.

The mounts filled every room in Brant's house. They cluttered the living room, dining room, basement, den and recreation room. Even the bedrooms were filled with assorted stuffed animals. To Halstead, it seemed as if he was walking through a forest of antlers and fangs.

Brant was proud of his collection. He pointed to a grand slam of North American sheep hanging on one wall of his bedroom. The grand slam consisted of the mounted heads of the four wild sheep species native to North America—the thin-horned Dall and stone, and the thick-horned desert bighorn and Rocky Mountain bighorn. "I got those from a woman in New York for less than $1,000," he boasted.

Brant was a strange individual with a peculiar hobby. He collected stuffed animals, acquiring new mounts like a stamp or coin collector acquires a new commemorative or proof set. He bought, sold and traded for stuffed animals—and turned a handsome profit on his hobby. Unlike big-game sportsmen, who frequently display the mounts of animals they have shot, Brant cared little for the chase, saying, "I only hunt white-tailed deer."

Brant owned a roadside truckstop which enabled him to finance his hobby. In one year, he said, he spent $24,000 for taxidermy work; money spent to acquire new trading stock, add new animals to his collection, and restore old mounts that showed signs of aging.

Halstead's initial contact with Brant had occurred two weeks earlier. Halstead called the collector, pretending to respond to an advertisement Brant had placed in a magazine offering to sell, trade, or buy mounted animals. Posing as a like-minded collector, Halstead had said, "I've got a leopard skin I'd like to trade for a tiger."

To Brant, who was used to such exchanges, the request was not in the least unusual. He swapped or sold animals every week. But there was a hitch.

"I don't have a tiger to trade at this time," Brant said. "And I don't have the extra cash at the moment to buy a tiger skin. I'd have to pay $1,200 for a skin, not to mention the cost of having it mounted." Yet, Brant sensed he could make a deal. "Listen, I've got elk and deer antlers for sale or trade. I've got elk and deer capes. I've got all kinds of stuff. I'm also interested in your leopard. Maybe we can make a deal. Why don't you come up here?"

Halstead promised to make the trip which triggered another question. "You haven't got a golden eagle, do you? I'm looking for a good mount of a golden eagle."

Brant was in an expansive mood when Halstead arrived at his house several weeks later. "I've got one of the largest private collections of mounted animals in existence," he boasted.

Halstead believed him. Never had he seen so many stuffed animals outside of a natural history museum. His mounts included not only North American game, but many foreign species as well. "If I don't have the animal you want, I can get it," Brant declared during Halstead's tour.

Halstead deliberately forgot to bring the leopard pelt he had mentioned over the phone, explaining to Brant he had been out of town on business for several days and did not carry it with him for fear of theft. This did not disturb Brant. Cash would be an acceptable substitute.

In the den, he pointed to a polar bear rug on the floor. "I can let you have that rug for $800. I've got another rug with the head attached that you can have for $1,700."

Nor did his sales pitch stop with the polar bears. "Everything here is for sale except the Marco Polo sheep and the full-mounted jaguar in the living room," he said.

He offered a pair of record-class mule deer antlers for $200, an elk head for $480, a set of average size elk antlers for $100. The African crowned cranes would cost $200, he said.

Halstead was dazed. The sale of many of the species Brant offered would constitute a violation of the law, he thought. The Endangered Species Act prohibits the sale of such animals as jaguars and leopards. The Marine Mammal Protection Act bans the trade in polar bears. Many states outlaw the sale of game animals, even heads of mounted game animals. The shipment of these species across state lines could violate the Lacey Act.

But precisely which laws Brant might be violating were of less importance at the moment than how Brant obtained so many different mounted animals and birds. Expressing astonishment over the scope of Brant's collection, Halstead asked, "How do you get all these animals?"

"I buy them from widows whose husbands were big game hunters. They don't like animals staring down at them from the walls. Most of them put the heads in the attic after their husbands die. I also buy them from taxidermists, and estate auctions. I find them in antique stores and at flea markets. But my best sources are zoos in Philadelphia and New York. I pay zookeepers who tip me off about dead animals or surplus ones which the zoo wants to get rid of. If the animal dies, I buy the pelt or head. If not, I buy it live and kill it to have it stuffed."

And, he hinted, for enough money, he could get a zookeeper to inject a deadly dose of poison into a prized specimen and then buy the carcass without raising any suspicions.

"Zoo animals are dying of natural and unexplained causes all the time," he noted. "Nobody raises an eyebrow over another dead animal. Besides, everybody in this business knows a dead animal is worth more than a live one."

Halstead, who was at this time running another undercover investigation into the illegal sale of eagles, listened with amazement. Then he said he would like to buy a bald eagle.

"I can't sell you an eagle," Brant replied. "I'm afraid to deal in them. The feds are too close. In fact, they busted one guy near here not too long ago for selling eagles." Indeed, it was a case made by Halstead. "But I will sell you a nice pair of stuffed owls," Brant said.

Halstead demurred, saying he would get back in touch. He left without buying anything. He had decided to bide his time. He was getting deeper and deeper into an investigation of the black market in eagles—a probe that was consuming more and more of his time. He wrote a memo to Washington, asking for a discreet check on Brant, a local taxidermist whose name Brant had mentioned, and the zoos in Philadelphia and New York concerning the disposal of live and dead animals.

Several weeks later, the intelligence section replied to Halstead's requests. Cursory investigations found nothing amiss with the zoos or the taxidermist, and little was known about Brant. He had been arrested three times—for killing a fawn out of season, for illegal possession of a fawn white-tailed deer, and for trespassing. Virtually nothing was known about his personal habits.

Halstead did not simply want to arrest Brant for selling, say, an owl. He wanted to discover the extent of the collector's activities and nab any other persons who might be involved, but there were no clues in the intelligence reports.

In October, Halstead requisitioned a jaguar pelt. The law enforcement division of the Fish and Wildlife Service has warehouses full of confiscated pelts and he wanted to use it as bait. With a young female agent posing as his daughter, he returned to Pennsylvania.

The two agents first stopped at the studio of the taxidermist whose name Brant had mentioned. Halstead told the taxidermist he wanted to buy a tiger or leopard pelt. The taxidermist brought a cardboard box out of a backroom. It contained two tiger pelts, a zebra hide, and a lion hide, all of which were for sale. The larger tiger hide, measuring 10-feet long, cost $1,500. The smaller hide, only 7 feet in length, cost $1,200. The zebra hide was priced at $300. "I've also got seal and polar bear hides," the taxidermist said while Halstead and his "daughter" examined the tiger and zebra pelts.

Halstead's partner, who shall be named Jennifer O'Malley, said she could not make up her mind which pelt she wanted. She wanted time to think about it. Halstead told the taxidermist they would get back in touch. They then drove to Brant's house, which was nearby.

Once again, Brant gave the agents a tour of his home, showing off his trophies. He had enormous numbers of mule deer, white-tailed deer and elk heads, which would be put to use during the upcoming hunting season. "Many of my customers are hunters who get skunked or who shoot a deer with only small, forked antlers. They will buy a big head to hang in their den or office, telling everybody this is the deer or elk they shot," he said.

Halstead attempted to persuade Brant to make a swap for the jaguar hide. But after Brant examined the yellow and black pelt, he handed it back to Halstead. "It's illegal to deal in jaguars," he said.

Halstead switched tactics, expressing interest in buying a stuffed white owl and a mounted head of a white-tailed deer.

"You can have both for $200," Brant said.

"I'll get back to you," Halstead replied.

O'Malley, Halstead's companion, called Brant the following week, saying she would mail a check from Halstead for $100 as down payment on the owl and deer head. The balance would be paid when the animals were picked up, probably within two weeks, she said.

Brant agreed with the arrangements.

Three weeks later, O'Malley returned to Pennsylvania. She carried with her a check from Halstead for the remaining $100. But O'Malley did not simply pick up the owl and deer head. She partied with Brant for three days—an amorous interlude marked by heavy drinking.

When Halstead called Brant several days later, the collector was noticeably cool. "I know who you are," he told Halstead. "You're a federal agent."

Halstead's cover had been blown by his fellow agent. Brant never was arrested and O'Malley quit the service soon afterward. Halstead later asked her why she spilled the beans to Brant.

"I felt sorry for him," she explained. Brant had won the heart of the lady.

The Goat Hunt

William Salinger, not his real name, gave only perfunctory attention to the two men who walked into his Idaho taxidermy studio one May afternoon. They said they were passing through on business, and had noted the huge elk antlers mounted out front of the studio. They wanted to inquire about trout fishing on the Salmon River and big game hunting in the Selway-Bitterroot wilderness area.

At first, Salinger provided only limited information. Scores of tourists passed through his shop asking the same questions, but few ever booked a hunting or fishing trip. But when Salinger sensed the two men were serious, he warmed to the request. He introduced himself and there was an exchange of business cards. Halstead's card identified him as Bob Hall, president of RBL Associates of Newark, Delaware. His companion, fellow agent Dave Kirkland, identified himself as Dave Straub, also of RBL, a fictitious firm supposedly engaged in the sale of heavy equipment.

"Fishing is no problem," Salinger explained. "Any nonresident can get a fishing license—and there are a few outfitters around here who will take you down the river on a float trip. But hunting is a different story. First of all, it depends on what you want to hunt. Elk hunts are easy to arrange—and the elk are big. You have a good chance to kill a record-class elk. Bear hunting is good, especially in the spring when they come out of hibernation. They are easy to kill at that time of year.

"As for mountain goats and sheep," Salinger continued "Well, that's a different matter. Goats generally are no problem. A few guides or outfitters

97

around here generally draw goat permits. You shoot the goat and use the guide's permit to make it appear legal. Bighorn sheep are an altogether different matter. It's almost impossible to get a hunting permit for bighorn, even for a resident hunter or outfitter. Your best bet is to hire someone who will take you down the Salmon River by jet-boat in late November after the regular sheep hunting season has closed. There are normally eight to ten big rams that are driven down to the river's edge by winter snows and you can shoot them from the boat. But this type of hunt is expensive. It costs around $1,000. And if you want the head mounted, I'd suggest you find a taxidermist back East. There's less chance of getting caught."

Halstead and Kirkland listened intently. They had come to Idaho at the request of the state's fish and game department, which was concerned about reports of Rocky Mountain bighorn sheep poaching along the Salmon River during the winter months. The department asked the U.S. Fish and Wildlife Service for assistance.

The taxidermy shop marked the first stop on their reconnaisance mission to the area suspected of being the center of the poaching.

When Salinger finished, Halstead promised to get back in touch. They left the studio and drove to a local bar, ordered a pair of draft beers, and engaged the bartender in conversation about big game hunting. The bartender directed them to a nearby sporting goods store for names of outfitters and guides. He emphasized that hunts could be arranged if a hunter was willing to spend the money.

Halstead and Kirkland stayed in town for two days, talking to anyone who would discuss big game hunting. The responses were always the same. They were assured of trophy animals if they brought plenty of cash.

The best source of information, however, appeared to be Salinger, the taxidermist. In Halstead's judgment, Salinger seemed to possess the best connections with local guides and outfitters. Moreover, since Salinger did not himself guide hunting parties, he was not in competition with other outfitters. He seemed to share their confidences.

Halstead decided that a third man should be brought into the undercover operation—a state game warden—a move designed to thwart any possible legal barriers.

The poaching problem stemmed primarily from too many hunters and too few hunting permits. Many western states conduct a lottery in late summer to issue hunting licenses for such species as goats and bighorn sheep. Thousands of hunters apply for the permits, but only a few names are drawn. State laws prohibit the transfer of the permit to another individual. Some of the activities mentioned by Salinger, such as selling a mountain goat permit, would not violate federal law but would be contrary to state law.

The man chosen to assist them was Darold Morgan, who was relatively unknown. He had been a game warden for only one year and the likelihood of being discovered was slim. He, too, was "employed" by the fictitious RBL Associates.

Morgan was given business cards showing him to be the "western representative" of RBL and the address listed on the card was a post office box in the state capital.

In a letter to Morgan, Neil T. Argy, the senior resident U.S. Fish and Wildlife Service agent in that area, explained the set-up—a procedure often used by U.S. Fish and Wildlife Service law enforcement agents. "The box number is fictitious," Argy wrote. "I have made arrangements with the postal inspector to intercept any mail coming to this box and to send it to my office. The phone number listed on your business card rings on my office phone and will be answered by Marilyn, my secretary. When this number rings, she will answer using the name RBL Associates, take the name and phone number of the person making the call, and then have you return the call."

In August, Halstead and Kirkland returned to nail down final arrangements for a hunting trip that fall. Salinger promised to set up an elk hunt for $60 a day.

"Can we get elk tags?" Halstead asked.

"Don't buy them right away," Salinger cautioned. "Wait until you kill an elk. Then come back into town and buy a tag."

"What are our chances for a mountain goat permit?"

"I'll have to check with Joe, but it probably won't be any problem," Salinger replied.

Halstead, Kirkland, the game warden Morgan, and Salinger were crowded into Halstead's room at a local motel. Halstead appeared impatient over the failure of Salinger to secure a goat permit. "Why don't you call him now?" he suggested.

Salinger picked up the phone. When his conversation ended, he looked at Halstead and said, "The goat tag will cost you $450. You understand that the person in whose name the tag is issued must go hunting with you, or at least be close by in case the game warden shows up."

Halstead nodded. "I see no problem with that. What about a sheep permit?"

"I think that will cost over $1,000, but we can work that out later. It's too early to plan for sheep," Salinger stated.

Two weeks later, Kirkland called Salinger. The state fish and game department had completed its lottery drawing for sheep and goat licenses. Over 6,000 hunters had applied for a sheep-hunting license; only 103 permits were issued. The sheep hunt appeared doomed.

"With no more permits than that, it'll be pretty hard to come up with a sheep permit, I'm afraid," Salinger told Kirkland. "There is no way to hunt sheep that I can see."

"If you could figure out any way for Bob to have a chance to hunt, that would be great, even if it's real late or whatever," Kirkland said. "Whatever you come up with is fine with us."

"Good enough," Salinger replied.

That conversation was one of several the agents had with Salinger during the summer—phone calls designed to show him they were still interested in the fall hunt. All the phone conversations were secretly taped for use as evidence in court.

In late October, the two agents returned. Salinger had found a man who was willing to sell the goat permit he had won in the lottery, but no sheep permits were for sale. The goat hunter was Joe Connors (not his real name), a tall, light-complected man in his early thirties. He made his living guiding hunters in the autumn and working at odd jobs the remainder of the year.

Connors walked into Halstead's motel room the night before the hunt was to begin. "I want $500 for my goat tag, plus $50-a-day guide fee," he said. "If we don't kill a goat, I want $100 per day." Halstead agreed to the terms.

Connors then returned a $200 check Halstead had sent him as a deposit for the hunt. "I want cash," he said. "I don't want any records of our transactions." Halstead apologized for the check, and promised to pay in cash.

Connors returned at six the following morning. Halstead and Kirkland got into Connors' four-wheel drive pick-up truck and headed southeast before turning off the highway and beginning a long climb up an old logging trail. "There usually are lots of goats in this area," Connors explained.

They parked the pick-up near the timberline, and walked for nearly three hours. They saw no goats in the rugged terrain.

"Let's move," Connors suggested. They got back into the pick-up and drove to another area near a creek. There they spotted a single goat on a ledge high above them. The shaggy-haired goat peered down at the hunters. It showed no alarm. The high mountain ledge was its security. Halstead and Kirkland paused to look closely at the goat through a spotting scope.

"He's too small," Halstead said.

Connors shrugged his shoulders. They moved off along the mountain. "There should be more goats later when we come back," he said.

Two and a half hours later, they returned to the spot where they had sighted the small goat, and spotted five other goats higher on the mountain. But all five were too distant to shoot. Then they spotted the small goat again.

"There's your goat. We had better kill it," Connors said. He was not bothered by the size of the goat. "We can get Salinger to fabricate the horns to make a good wall mount," he said. "The horns will be plenty big when he gets through with them."

The three men shouldered their rifles and took aim at the small white goat peering down at them from a ledge, perhaps 1,000 feet above them. Neither Halstead nor Kirkland wanted to kill the goat. They aimed high. Connors did not. The white goat tumbled off the ledge and fell in a great sweeping arc toward the creek below.

Connors and Kirkland climbed down the mountainside to the creek. Halstead waited by the pick-up truck.

When the two approached the goat, Connors shook his head sadly. One horn had been broken off in the fall, but that wasn't what bothered him. "It's too small," he said. "There is no way it can be mounted or made into a rug without people knowing it was a very young goat. We'll leave it here."

The young goat weighed about 60 pounds, Kirkland estimated when he picked it up. A mature billy sometimes will weigh close to 300 pounds. Kirkland dropped the goat, and the two men climbed back up the slope to Connors' pick-up truck.

Halstead and Kirkland hunted with Connors for two more days. They hunted several creek areas but they saw no goats. Connors, however, was not discouraged.

"Salinger and I poached the goat that's mounted and hanging at a sporting goods store in town. We killed it and left it in the field until nearly midnight, then went back in and packed it out. The sheep head hanging at a bar in town is one that I killed. I'd like to sell it for $1,500."

Halstead asked about hunting bighorn sheep; Connors said it could be arranged. "The best time would be in late December when the sheep are down along the river bottoms. But it will cost at least $2,000."

Halstead and Kirkland left without finding a trophy-sized goat. Unknown to Connors, they had called a local game warden the evening after their first day's hunting. The game warden retrieved the young goat Connors had shot for court evidence.

The goat was one piece of evidence, the secretly taped phone conversations were another, yet Halstead was uneasy. He had misgivings about the likelihood of a conviction, and when the case came to trial he was proved right.

What had worried him was that, despite all the effort he and Kirkland had put into the investigation, there simply wasn't enough solid evidence. Still, he told himself he could count on the secret tapes. Their quality wasn't all he had hoped for, but he felt the conversations of the previous summer were sufficiently intelligible—and incriminating—and of course they had been transcribed for careful courtroom examination.

He was shocked to learn later that all charges eventually had been dismissed on the grounds that the tapes contained gaps—dead spaces which made it seem that someone had tampered with the evidence.

He had learned long ago that you can't win them all. Some cases are doomed to end in frustration and bewilderment. Perhaps the state's enforcement personnel or someone on the prosecutor's staff had inadvertently damaged or erased portions in the course of reviewing the tapes. Halstead didn't know, nor was he ever able to find out. To this day, he knows only that the case was a bitter disappointment. But such disappointments go with the job of undercover investigation, and perhaps they make the victories all the more satisfying.

Reminiscences

During the course of his twenty-nine years in the U.S. Fish and Wildlife Service, Halstead worked on literally scores of investigations. It was not uncommon for him to be involved in several cases simultaneously, and at one point, he found himself juggling twenty-six different assignments at one time. Any kind of law enforcement work is often frustrating, and undercover work is inherently risky. Halstead knew that any innocent remark, any idle slip of the tongue, could not only jeopardize an investigation, but could put him in physical danger as well.

But it was not all frustration and danger. Over the years, Halstead ran into more than his share of oddball characters and weird, often funny, cases.

•   •   •

October 1, 1965, the opening day of the waterfowl hunting season in Maine. Tipped that several ponds in remote pine woods were being illegally baited with corn, authorities brought in several out-of-state agents, including Halstead, to launch a crackdown. In addition to salting the ponds with corn to illegally attract ducks, the hunters were reportedly killing excessive numbers of birds, especially black ducks and wood ducks.

Halstead found his assigned pond before daylight, hid in the bushes and waited. At first light he saw a hunter approach—a nattily attired man carrying a double-barreled Purdy shotgun. He was, Halstead would learn later, a Britisher. He wore a tweed shooting jacket with leather elbow patches and a snap-brim cap, and he was accompanied by a large black Labrador retriever.

The hunter erected a makeshift brush blind beside the water's edge and waited for the morning flight. It was not long in coming. As a flock of woodies swirled down from the sky, the hunter raised his shotgun and fired. One woodie fell and the dog leaped into the water and swam out to the downed bird.

But the Labrador refused to return the duck to the hunter. Instead, it mouthed the duck and swam back to shore some distance away. It walked directly toward Halstead, who was still hiding in the bushes. The dog stopped several yards in front of Halstead and ate the duck—a cardinal sin for a hunting dog.

Halstead suppressed a chuckle.

The hunter at first paid no attention to the dog's antics and continued shooting. He was a good shot; he quickly downed three more woodies, and each time, the dog would swim out and then return to its station in front of Halstead and chew up the ducks.

Soon, the hunter left his blind to search out the dog and retrieve his ducks. When he saw the remains of the dog's meal he said in a clipped accent, "You beastly critter, you're eating my ducks. I think I should kill you."

Then he looked up—and found himself looking right into Halstead's eyes. But Halstead realized he could not arrest the man. The dog had destroyed the evidence.

• • • •

One occasionally reads about a criminal who was caught red-handed. Halstead once caught a man red-mouthed.

In parts of rural North Carolina, robin stew is considered a delicacy. Yes, stew made from the same red-breasted birds that pull earthworms from your front lawn and signal the beginning of Spring.

The technique of hunting robins is simple. The hunters wait for a cold spell. This forces the birds to congregate heavily in roosts, frequently perching shoulder-to-shoulder (or wing-to-wing) on tree limbs in an effort to keep warm. At these times, the birds are especially vulnerable.

Halstead had received a tip about robin hunters near Rockingham. He waited until dark before moving into the area where the hunters were operating.

He found one man almost immediatey. He was clubbing the roost with a 12-foot wooden pole. He thrashed the lower limbs, knocking the shivering robins to the ground, where he picked them up and stuffed them into a gunny sack.

His partner used a different approach. He climbed into the trees and shined a flashlight into the birds' faces, momentarily blinding them. He grabbed the birds with one hand, then bit off their heads and tossed them into another gunny sack. When Halstead ordered him down out of the tree, he saw robin blood dripping off the man's lips and chin.

• • •

Once, Halstead discovered the sad fact that some law enforcement officers can be quite selective when deciding which laws they themselves will obey. They also do not like being caught.

In a crackdown on waterfowl poaching, Halstead had been ordered to Long Island. Among those he arrested were several New York City policemen who had been hunting without licenses and killing protected species. When he returned to his car, Halstead found it filled with new phonograph records. Suspecting a frame-up attempt, he refused to touch the car. He believed the cops had stashed stolen merchandise in his auto in order to teach him a lesson. Halstead called the local sheriff, who took the records from the car.

• • • •

A cold front had moved in, sealing parts of Currituck Sound with ice. Halstead was on routine automobile patrol with Ab Sumrell, a deputy U.S. game warden. They were about to pull into the Point Harbor Grill to have lunch when they noticed a small 15-foot sailboat heading southward down the sound. Three men were on board.

"You know that boat?" Halstead asked Sumrell.

"It doesn't belong on this side," he replied.

"Where do you think it will land?"

"On the Dare County side," Sumrell said.

On a hunch, they decided to check it out. They got into a jeep belonging to Jack Balance, a state game warden who was joining them for lunch. They drove across the bridge at Point Harbor and followed a long narrow trail across the sand dunes to a natural, protected harbor. The sailboat arrived about the same time.

Three men wearing hip boots got out of the anchored craft and waded toward shore. Each man carried a burlap bag over his shoulder. The six men met on the beach.

"What's in the bags?" Halstead asked.

"None of your goddam business," one man said.

Halstead could see where blood had soaked through one of the bags. The three wardens focused on the man carrying this bag.

They escorted him to Balance's jeep. When they attempted to open the bag, the man began fighting, ripping the canvas sides and top of the jeep in a futile struggle to escape. After handcuffing the man, Halstead held the burlap bag upside down and gave it a shake. Out fell a dead whistling swan. The wardens found a second dead swan in another bag. The third bag contained dirty clothes.

The three men turned out to be marsh guards for a private hunting club, hired to keep other hunters off the property. They were returning home for the weekend—carrying their dirty clothes and two swans for Sunday dinner.

•   •   •   •

The man had been illegally gunning shorebirds. After a chase and a brief scuffle, Halstead had arrested the man. Now, they were returning from the barrier island to the mainland aboard a coast guard boat. Halstead had placed one handcuff on the poacher's wrist and one handcuff on his own wrist.

Soon, the poacher's relatives came alongside in a smaller, faster craft. "Jump, Jimmy!" they yelled. "We'll get you!"

It was an obvious attempt to effect an escape. They would pluck Jimmy from the water and outrun the slower coast guard boat. But Jimmy did not jump.

"I can't jump," he cried out. "I'm handcuffed to this big son of a bitch!"

•   •   •   •

Halstead retired in 1977, after twenty-nine years with the U.S. Fish and Wildlife Service. He now spends his time hunting, fishing and trapping near his home in Newark, Delaware, and at his cabin in Maine where he spends his summers.